Letters of Grace & Beauty

Reading the Bible as Literature

How Bible Stories Work: A Guided Study of Biblical Narrative

Sweeter Than Honey, Richer Than Gold: A Guided Study of Biblical Poetry

Letters of Grace & Beauty: A Guided Literary Study of New Testament Epistles

Jesus the Hero: A Guided Literary Study of the Gospels

Symbols & Reality: A Guided Study of Prophecy, Apocalypse, and Visionary Literature

Short Sentences Long Remembered: A Guided Study of Proverbs and Other Wisdom Literature

READING
THE BIBLE AS
LITERATURE

Letters of Grace & Beauty

A GUIDED LITERARY STUDY
OF NEW TESTAMENT EPISTLES

LELAND RYKEN

LEXHAM PRESS

Letters of Grace & Beauty: A Guided Literary Study of New Testament Epistles
© 2016 by Leland Ryken

Lexham Press, 1313 Commercial St., Bellingham, WA 98225
LexhamPress.com

First edition by Weaver Book Company.

Verse numbers appear in Scripture quotations because the author sometimes refers to or comments on specific verses.

Print ISBN 9781683591566
Digital ISBN 9781683591573

Cover design and interior layout: Frank Gutbrod

Contents

Series Preface   9

Introduction:
The New Testament Epistles as a Genre   13

What Is an Epistle?   14
Who Wrote the Epistles, and Why?   15
How Literary Are the Epistles?   16
How Have the Epistles Been Misrepresented to Us?   17
Summary   18

1. **Types of New Testament Letters**   19
Letter Writing in General   20
The Basic Paradigm of New Testament Epistles   22
Circular Letters   23
Personal Letters   25
Family Letters and Letters of Friendship   26
Letter-Essays   27
Missionary Letters   28
Administrative or Official Letters   29
LEARNING BY DOING   31

2. **Literary Genres from the Broader World of Literature**   33
Occasional Literature   33

Diatribe 36
Autobiography 39
Farewell Discourse 40
LEARNING BY DOING 42

3. **Opening and Closing in New Testament Epistles** 43
   Openings 44
       The Elements of the Opening 44
       Purpose of the Opening 46
       Effect of the Opening 47
       Adaptation of Classical Openings 47
       Implications for Reading and Interpretation 48
       A Model for Our Own Letters 49
   LEARNING BY DOING 49
   Closings 50
       Final Greeting and Benediction 50
       Added Material 51
       Implications for Reading and Interpretation 52
   LEARNING BY DOING 53

4. **The Thanksgiving in the Letters of the New Testament** 55
   Structure 56
   Content 57
   Function or Effect 58
   Implications for Interpretation and Teaching 59
   LEARNING BY DOING 60

5. **Paraenesis: Walking Worthy of the Lord** 63
   General Considerations 63
   Defining Paraenesis 65
   Interpreting Paraenesis 66
   Household Codes 68
   Why Paraenesis? 69
   LEARNING BY DOING 70

6. **Body: Giving Shape to New Testament Epistles** 73
   Instruction or Exposition 74
   Command 76
   Exhortation 76
   Persuasion 77
   Autobiography 78
   Praise and Rebuke 79
   Prayer and Request 80
   Summary 80
   LEARNING BY DOING 81

7. **Organization and Structure of New Testament Letters** 83
   Fallacies 83
   Review of Principles Previously Covered 85
   The Structure of Thought and Feeling 86
   LEARNING BY DOING 88

8. **Embedded Genres within New Testament Epistles** 89
   Lists of Virtues and Vices 89
   Doxology and Benediction 91
   Christ Hymn 92
   Encomium 93
   Church Manual and Pastoral Handbook 93
   Travelogue 94
   LEARNING BY DOING 96

9. **Style of the Letters of the New Testament** 97
   Poetry and Figurative Language 98
   High Style in the Epistles 100
   Plain Style in the Epistles 103
   Aphoristic Style 105
   LEARNING BY DOING 106

Afterword 109

Series Preface

This series is part of the mission of the publisher to equip Christians to understand and teach the Bible effectively by giving them reliable tools for handling the biblical text. Within that landscape, the niche that my volumes are designed to fill is the literary approach to the Bible. This has been my scholarly passion for nearly half a century. It is my belief that a literary approach to the Bible is the common reader's friend, in contrast to more specialized types of scholarship on the Bible.

Nonetheless, the literary approach to the Bible needs to be defended against legitimate fears by evangelical Christians, and through the years I have not scorned to clear the territory of misconceptions as part of my defense of a literary analysis of the Bible. In kernel form, my message has been this:

1. To view the Bible as literature is not a suspect modern idea, nor does it need to imply theological liberalism. The idea of the Bible as literature began with the writers of the Bible, who display literary qualities in their writings and who refer with technical precision to a wide range of literary genres such as psalm, proverb, parable, apocalypse, and many more.

2. Although fiction is a common trait of literature, it is not an essential feature of it. A work of literature can be replete with literary technique and artifice while remaining historically factual.

3. To approach the Bible as literature need not be characterized by viewing the Bible *only* as literature, any more than reading it as history requires us to see only the history of the Bible.

4. When we see literary qualities in the Bible we are not attempting to bring the Bible down to the level of ordinary literature; it is simply an objective statement about the inherent nature of the Bible. The Bible can be trusted to reveal its extraordinary qualities if we approach it with ordinary methods of literary analysis.

To sum up, it would be tragic if we allowed ourselves to be deprived of literary methods of analyzing the Bible by claims that are fallacies.

What, then, does it mean to approach the Bible as literature? A literary study of the Bible should begin where any other approach begins—by accepting as true all that the biblical writers claim about their book. These claims include its inspiration and superintendence by God, its infallibility, its historical truthfulness, its unique power to infiltrate people's lives, and its supreme authority.

With that as a foundation, a literary approach to the Bible is characterized by the following traits:

1. An acknowledgement that the Bible comes to us in a predominantly literary format. In the words of C. S. Lewis, "There is a . . . sense in which the Bible, since it is after all literature, cannot properly be read except as literature; and the different parts of it as the different sorts

of literature they are."[1] The overall format of the Bible is that of an anthology of literature.

2. In keeping with that, a literary approach identifies the genres and other literary forms of the Bible and analyzes individual texts in keeping with those forms. An awareness of literary genres and forms programs how we analyze a biblical text and opens doors into a text that would otherwise remain closed.

3. A literary approach begins with the premise that a work of literature embodies universal human experience. Such truthfulness to human experience is complementary to the tendency of traditional approaches to the Bible to mainly see ideas in it. A literary approach corrects a commonly held fallacy that the Bible is a theology book with proof texts attached.

4. A literary approach to the Bible is ready to grant value to the biblical authors' skill with language and literary technique, seeing these as an added avenue to our enjoyment of the Bible.

5. A literary approach to the Bible takes its humble place alongside the two other main approaches—the theological and the historical. These three domains are established by the biblical writers themselves, who usually combine all three elements in their writings. However, in terms of space, the Bible is a predominantly literary book. Usually the historical and theological material is packaged in literary form.

These traits and methods of literary analysis govern the content of my series of guided studies to the genres of the Bible.

---

1   *Reflections on the Psalms* (New York: Harcourt, Brace & World, 1958), 3.

Although individual books in my series are organized by the leading literary genres that appear in the Bible, I need to highlight that all of these genres have certain traits in common. Literature itself, en masse, makes up a homogenous whole. In fact, we can speak of *literature as a genre* (the title of the opening chapter of a book titled *Kinds of Literature*). The traits that make up literature as a genre will simply be assumed in the volumes in this series. They include the following: universal, recognizable human experience concretely embodied as the subject matter; the packaging of this subject matter in distinctly literary genres; the authors' use of special resources of language that set their writing apart from everyday expository discourse; stylistic excellence and other forms of artistry that are part of the beauty of a work of literature.

What are the advantages that come from applying the methods of literary analysis? In brief, they are as follows: an improved method of interacting with biblical texts in terms of the type of writing that they are; doing justice to the specificity of texts (again because the approach is tailored to the genres of a text); ability to see unifying patterns in a text; relating texts to everyday human experience; enjoyment of the artistic skill of biblical authors.

Summary

A book needs to be read in keeping with its author's intention. We can see from the Bible itself that it is a thoroughly literary book. God superintended its authors to write a very (though not wholly) literary book. To pay adequate attention to the literary qualities of the Bible not only helps to unlock the meanings of the Bible; it is also a way of honoring the literary intentions of its authors. Surely biblical authors regarded everything that they put into their writing as important. We also need to regard those things as important.

Introduction

The New Testament Epistles as a Genre

Over the course of my half-century career as a specialist in the Bible as literature, the genre on which my understanding has changed most is the epistle. The more I have learned about the genre (most recently in a book of literary introductions to the individual books of the Bible), the more excited I have become about the epistles as literature. I need to flag the phrase "as literature." Most seminary-trained ministers would be content to preach solely from the epistles, but their interest is all theological and not at all literary. The seed for this non-literary approach is planted by biblical scholars.

This guided study to the epistles is part of a series that explores the literary genres of the Bible. This means that my approach to the epistles will focus on the literary forms that we find in them rather than their theological content. I also need to explain that I will survey the epistles as a group; this book does not attempt to do what can only be accomplished with literary introductions to the individual New Testament epistles. Along those lines, I encourage my readers to take a look at three of my previously published books: *Ryken's Bible Handbook* (Wheaton, IL: Tyndale, 2005); *Literary Study Bible* (Wheaton, IL: Crossway, 2007); and *Literary Introductions to the Books of the Bible* (Wheaton, IL: Crossway, 2015).

To give shape to this introduction to the New Testament epistles, I have packaged my material as answers to a series of questions.

What Is an Epistle?

An epistle is a letter. I will use the terms "epistle" and "letter" interchangeably in this guide. Nonetheless, I will do so in awareness that the two terms have different connotations. Both sets of associations are helpful, and by themselves the two terms are incomplete as labels for the New Testament genre known as an epistle.

The word "epistle" implies a letter that is different from the letters and emails that we ordinarily write. An epistle is more formal in vocabulary and style than an ordinary letter. The term also implies a letter that is public rather than purely personal. Additionally, an epistle is assumed to be more literary (however defined) than the letters we ourselves write, and the content resembles that of a teaching ("didactic") document more than a letter that conveys only personal news and feelings.

All of these traits are characteristic of the epistles, as we will see. The epistles were largely intended for public audiences (even when the original recipient was a single person like Timothy). The authors show an awareness that they were writing for posterity, and not only for the immediate recipients of their letters. The New Testament epistles are rhetorically embellished and sophisticated in technique. The style is often elevated far above the idiom of the dormitory and bus stop.

But there are other aspects of the New Testament epistles that make them better labeled as letters than epistles. The style is not uniformly embellished and formal; many passages read exactly like what we might write in a letter or say in a telephone conversation. Similarly with the content of the epistles: many passages in these letters resemble what we ourselves would say in a letter, such as the parting travel information or requests to pass on greetings to mutual acquaintances that we find at the close of the New Testament epistles.

This informal side often gets ignored and misrepresented (with results that will be noted below), and perhaps the term "epistle" aids and abets this misrepresentation. I will use the terms "epistle" and "letter" interchangeably as a way of keeping both the formal and informal aspects of the letters in view.

Who Wrote the Epistles, and Why?

The epistles were written in the second half of the first century. Some scholars place the epistles under the heading of "early Christian literature," or "the literature of the early Christian movement." These are appropriate and helpful labels. The epistles, along with the rest of the New Testament, were the first writings of the early Christian church. We can accurately think of these writings as "founding documents" of the Christian movement.

The authors of the epistles were the apostles designated by Christ to be his spokesmen and the official guardians of what he taught. They were ordinary people divinely set apart for the task of recording the facts about Christ's earthly life (chiefly in the Gospels) and the theological meaning of that life. The latter is the domain of the epistles. An apostle speaks with a unique authority, and we are continuously aware of this as we read the epistles. In particular, Paul, who was not a disciple of Jesus but was called to be an apostle nonetheless, regularly appeals to his apostolic authority in his letters.

Why did the apostles write the epistles? The answers are multiple. Certainly they wrote to impart theological information about the Christian faith. But they had other goals in additional to informing the minds of readers. Many of the passages are slanted toward exhorting readers to live in accordance with what they know. In fact, many of the epistles have a doctrinal first half, followed by a practical second half that tells readers how to live based on the doctrine that has been presented. In addition to the exhortations (a hortatory purpose), we find passages that are persuasive and emotional in nature, urging and moving readers to live in a certain way (a persuasive purpose and not only hortatory). Finally, there is a prevailing doxological ("having the intention to praise") purpose in the epistles.

How Literary Are the Epistles?

We do not need the foregoing information about the authors of the epistles and their intentions to know that the epistles are uniquely powerful. I will speak personally in this regard. I have been pained to see the propensity of preachers to gravitate so automatically to the epistles to the neglect of the rest of the Bible. Furthermore, in theory the epistles are less literary (and more expository) than the rest of the literary parts of the Bible. To my surprise, therefore, I find that I know the epistles better than other parts of the Bible, and the aphorisms (memorable sayings) that stick in my memory come to a disproportionate degree from the epistles. This is a tribute to the hidden literary brilliance of the epistles, and this guided study is an attempt to explain that literary quality.

In my early writings on the Bible as literature (e.g., my 1974 book *How to Read the Bible as Literature*), I included chapters or units on the New Testament epistles only for the sake of being complete and not omitting a genre that my readers were expecting me to include. I viewed the epistles as more expository than literary in form. They did not strongly awaken my literary interest. But the closer I look at the epistles and take stock of their impact on me, the more literary they seem. What features make up this literary dimension?

I will start with the observation that prose is capable of being literary. Courses in English and American literature usually include prose works (and not only in the form of novels and plays). The chosen works and passages are subjected to literary analysis for their style and technique, and these are regarded as artistically self-rewarding. Much of the prose that we find in the epistles corresponds to that, and in saying that the aesthetic beauty of the writing is self-rewarding I do not intend to exclude the other dimensions (including the theological and moral content) that we value in the epistles.

Although exposition of theology and exhortation to godly living are the purposes that moved the writers of the epistles, they wrote with such an amazing grasp of literary technique that to ignore this aspect of the epistles is to distort them. In fact, any in-depth analysis of *what* the epistles communicate leads naturally to an awareness of *how* they communicate that content. This guided study will explore the "how" of communication in the epistles.

How Have the Epistles Been Misrepresented to Us?

I would prefer not to write this section of the chapter, but I do not believe this to be an option. One misrepresentation of the epistles has been the impression that many ministers convey that the epistles are the most important section of the Bible and virtually the only essential part of the Bible for Christians. There has been an overemphasis on the epistles in many evangelical circles, to the neglect of other biblical genres.

That is the beginning of woes. To add to the problem, the epistles are typically approached in a manner that is not in keeping with the kind of writing they are. I remember how shocked I was when a minister said as a kind of aside, "The epistles are really sermons." As with a camera click, the picture came into focus for me. "Oh," I said to myself, "*that* is why ministers mishandle the epistles, and in the specific ways that they do."

The epistles are rightly named: they are epistles or letters. They do not closely resemble any sermon that is preached from the pulpit. Nor are the epistles essays or treatises in the familiar sense. I have grown discontent with the approach that imposes a melodic line on the epistles because it is reductionistic and enforces an ideational unity on the epistles that they do not in fact possess.

Even more objectionable is biblical scholars' practice of imposing a strictness of coherence on the epistles that exceeds anything that they themselves have ever written (including their dissertations). The epistles are as disjointed in structure and wide-ranging in topics as the letters that we ourselves write. They are not a seamless flow of thought from one paragraph to the next. Instead they have the flow of a letter.

Summary

The epistles are a literary paradox. They are so theological and moral in subject matter that they lull us into thinking that they are purely expository and informational in nature. But along with this obvious feature we find an abundance of literary technique. These literary forms are what embody the theological and moral meanings, and they contribute to the forcefulness of utterance that we experience with the epistles. The literary flair of the authors can also add a dimension of enjoyment to our reading of the epistles.

Types of
New Testament Letters

The game plan for this book is to begin with two chapters that provide a broad picture of letter writing in the New Testament. Then the focus will narrow to more specific components of the epistles. The first two chapters should be viewed as providing a framework within which later chapters will be placed.

A preliminary consideration for this chapter is that the epistles belong to a broader category that is common in the Bible. Literary scholars call it the "mixed-genre format," and they also speak of "encyclopedic form." This means that a passage or book of the Bible does not display the traits of just one genre but of multiple ones. We can accurately think of the New Testament epistles as hybrids that combine multiple genres, literary forms, and styles. Sometimes it is helpful to think of these genres as overlapping (such as a personal letter that is simultaneously an autobiography), but in other instances it is more helpful to think of them as existing side by side (such as an opening section of theological exposition followed by a unit of moral exhortation).

All of the epistles fall into the genre of the letter, with the result that a preliminary set of considerations automatically kicks in for all of the epistles. But there are more letter types than simply the generic one, and one or more of these is always capable of entering a New Testament epistle. Sometimes the general category "letter" with its five standard elements suffices as a description of a given epistle, but usually something more is needed. The current chapter aims to provide a menu of types of letters that we find in the New Testament epistles.

A final preliminary point is very important: in almost no instance does a New Testament epistle fall *completely* into a given category. It would therefore be wrong to think of a letter as being only a personal letter, for example, or only a letter of friendship. The operative principle is that the New Testament epistles do not always fall completely into this or that genre but instead *show affinities with or resemblances to* the epistolary genres that I cover in this chapter. The explanatory value of having this menu of genres at our disposal is immense, but we need to avoid looking for a single rubric and then forcing the entire letter into that mold. I will note in passing that the reason I do not use the categories of classical rhetoric such as deliberative rhetoric and judicial rhetoric or epideictic rhetoric is that the rhetorical approach has been extremely guilty of forcing individual epistles into just one category and confusing readers as a result.

Letter Writing in General

One reason the New Testament epistles have been misrepresented is that people do not take time to consider the genre of the letter as they themselves know and practice it. Everyone has some experience with letters. It is true that the electronic age has made the letter a somewhat neglected and forgotten form, but this is counteracted if we include emails as a form of letter writing.

What things characterize our own letters? They are a form of communication, first of all, designed to convey information of many potential types from the writer to the recipient. Sometimes the information is the whole point of the letter, but on other occasions there is an element of persuasion as well. Or there may be an emotional component, as the writer aims to convey not only information but feelings such as love or anger. Sometimes the information focuses on conditions or ideas that exist objectively, quite apart from the writer of the letter, but on other occasions a letter conveys personal information about the writer, or personal responses to a situation. In all these ways, the content of letters is varied and multiple, and already we can see that the common practice of reducing New Testament epistles to a single topic or purpose is misleading.

What about the form and organization of the letters we write and receive? Well, how many times have we sat down to write a letter by formulating a thesis and an outline of topic sentences under it? Probably never. That paradigm is the format of an essay, and letters are not essays. In how many of our letters do we carefully compose a topic sentence for every paragraph? Rarely. How often do we stop while composing a letter and say, "Wait a minute—that unit does not fit the melodic line of my letter?" How often do we compose a transition paragraph between two paragraphs that deal with sharply different subject matter, or make sure that there is a seamless flow of logic from one paragraph to the next?

A lot of harm has been done by overlooking the obvious and by imposing criteria on the New Testament epistles that belong to essays rather than letters. The Roman author Seneca, who lived at approximately the same time as the New Testament writers, said regarding his letters that they "should be just what my conversation would be if you and I were sitting in one another's company or taking walks together." That is not the *whole* truth about letter writing, but it is an important *part* of the truth.

We can summarize what characterizes letter writing in general as follows, realizing that a given letter might be a partial exception:

- Most letters cover multiple topics, not just one.
- Letters are not organized like an essay with a thesis sentence, subordinate generalizations under that thesis, and topic sentences for every paragraph.
- The main principle of organization is a series of self-contained paragraphs (we tend to "think paragraph" as we compose a letter).
- The linear organization of a letter is free-flowing and informal; we take up topics as they occur to us.
- As a result, the flow from one paragraph to the next is often disjointed.

The foregoing list is descriptive of letters generally and is not offered as prescriptive or something that is always followed.

The Basic Paradigm of New Testament Epistles

The New Testament epistles resemble (but are not identical with) letter-writing conventions in the ancient world (and scholars often use the formulas *Greco-Roman* and *classical* for my adjective *ancient*). Letters in the ancient world followed a basic three-part paradigm: introduction or salutation, body, and closing. The New Testament epistles have those parts, too, but two ingredients were added to complete the format and make the New Testament epistles distinctive. The resulting template is as follows:

- salutation (sender, recipient, greeting)
- thanksgiving
- body
- paraenesis (section of commands)
- closing

A few qualifications need to be made. Some epistles omit one or more of these elements. Although the order noted above is the norm, the order might be slightly rearranged, or a given element might appear more than once in a letter. Additionally, even though the body is nearly always the dominant ingredient, with the thanksgiving and paraenesis taking up only limited space, sometimes one of those elements assumes a major role in a given letter. The constancy of the paradigm shows that the New Testament writers composed their epistles within an accepted understanding of their genre.

Anyone who wishes to see what this five-part format looks like with a specific epistle can take time now to read or browse the book of Ephesians. Here is an outline that applies the grid:

- salutation: sender, recipient, greeting (1:1–2)
- thanksgiving: the spiritual riches that the recipients possess and prayer for their spiritual welfare (1:3–23)
- body of the letter (2:1–4:16)
- paraenesis, or list of exhortations (4:17–6:20)
- closing: information on how the letter will be delivered and concluding benediction (6:21–24)

Circular Letters

A circular letter is a letter intended for circulation among a group of people. Often the salutation or close in such a letter signals the group that is envisioned, but this is not a requirement. Because the easiest way to circulate a letter is to read it orally to an assembled group, this is frequently how circular letters are disseminated. We should note that both the Old and New Testaments belong to what are called oral cultures, meaning that documents were more likely to be read aloud and heard than read silently and privately.

Certain features of letters fall into place when we picture them as circular letters. For example, a kind of universality descends on them, both for the first recipients and for us as we read them hundreds of years later. We sense that what we are reading applies to all Christians in all times. Balancing this universality, we can exercise our historical imagination and picture ourselves as being present at a reading of an epistle in a church service. We realize that the writer is not addressing us personally but a whole group. In a circular letter, the issues discussed are likely to be of public concern.

Certain qualities of the genre of the circular letter are *automatically* present as we read the New Testament epistles, while other features emerge with more clarity if we become self-consciously aware of the communal aspect. We sense *intuitively* that there is a foundational and normative quality to the New Testament epistles, and that the writers are laying down guidelines for the future of the church to the end of time. But we have an even firmer reason to regard them in this light when we are consciously aware that these letters are more than individual messages addressed only to original recipients or to us. They are church documents addressed to whole congregations and ultimately to the church worldwide. The more widely a circular letter is disseminated, the better, whereas we read personal letters addressed to someone else with at least a slight sense that we are intruding on something private.

The first tip-off that the New Testament epistles were intended as circular letters is their titles: Romans, Ephesians, Philippians, Colossians. These titles name groups residing in a specified city or region. This, in turn, implies an oral culture in which even the epistles that are addressed to individuals (Timothy, Titus, Philemon) convey the impression that these letters are intended for the church universal and not simply for the solitary addressee. For example, the letter to Philemon is a letter of request addressed to a specific person and situation, and yet the opening salutation addresses not only Philemon but also "the church in your house" (v. 2).

The following salutations from selected New Testament epistles confirm what has been said:

- "To all those in Rome who are loved by God and called to be saints" (Rom. 1:7).
- "To the church of God that is in Corinth, . . . together with all those who in every place call upon the name of our Lord Jesus Christ" (1 Cor. 1:2).
- "To all the saints in Christ Jesus who are at Philippi with the overseers and deacons" (Phil. 1:1).

Personal Letters

As applied to the New Testament epistles, the designation "personal letter" denotes multiple things. Sometimes it identifies letters that are addressed to individuals rather than groups. The epistles that fit this definition are those addressed to Timothy, Titus, and Philemon. We cannot get much mileage out of the designation *personal* for these letters, though, because even these epistles have served a normative purpose in the church and in the case of 1 Timothy and Titus have been used as church manuals.

A second definition of a personal letter is a letter in which the writer shares a lot of personal information about himself or herself. Of course every New Testament epistle was written by an individual person, but the epistles vary widely in the amount of personal information they contain. The more such information that we find, the more natural it becomes to think of an epistle as a personal letter, as contrasted to a public letter dealing with issues external to the writer.

None of the New Testament epistles is only a personal letter, but in some of them the writer shares a large amount of personal information and personal feelings. In these cases the concept introduced above of overlapping genres is helpful, as the concept of a personal letter merges with other genres.

Family Letters and Letters of Friendship

Two genres that often overlap with the personal letter are the family letter and the letter of friendship. In fact, only under special circumstances would we write a personal letter to someone other than a family member or friend. Family letters and letters of friendship were well-established epistolary genres in the ancient world.

Family letters are addressed to members of a family. The content of such a letter touches upon family relationships and information pertaining to family life. The tone is familial, emotional, and affectionate.

There are no pure examples of family letters in the New Testament, but some of the epistles have affinities with family letters. For example, several of the epistles speak of the church under the metaphor of a family. As an extension of that, the writers often refer to individual fellow Christians as their brother, sister, or child. Here are two random examples: "To Timothy, my true child in the faith" (1 Tim. 1:2); "to Apphia our sister" (Philem. 2). Most conclusively of all, the stock address to "brothers" or "brothers and sisters" occurs approximately 125 times in the combined epistles. The overtones of the family letter are simply part of what we bring to a reading of the epistles.

The letter of friendship is only slightly less prominent. For starters, whenever Paul shares personal information or feelings, we naturally assimilate these references as a friend speaking to friends. But certain conventional ingredients of the letter of friendship make the case even stronger. Here is a brief list of traits in a letter of friendship, whether in antiquity or today: (1) naming the recipients either as individuals or a group; (2) references to shared experiences, either past or present; (3) friendship offered as the basis for a request; (4) expression of feelings that are part of friendship; (5) statements of longing to be present with the recipients. All of these are common in the epistles.

Letter-Essays

The use of the word "essay" here should not be construed to mean that I have abandoned my earlier disclaimer that the New Testament epistles are not essays. Two New Testament epistles (Romans and Hebrews) fall decisively into the category of letter-essay, and neither of them strongly resembles essays such as we ourselves write and read. Nonetheless, they contain a preponderance of theological exposition and thereby possess some of the qualities of an essay more than a typical letter. The label *didactic letter* ("teaching letter") is a helpful related category, though virtually all of the New Testament epistles have a teaching element without falling into the genre of letter-essay.

In a letter-essay, the usual epistolary conventions take a back seat to the essay element. For example, the book of Romans follows the conventions of letter writing only at the beginning and end. The opening fifteen verses are a thoroughly familiar salutation and thanksgiving, and the last chapter reads just like the closing of other New Testament epistles. But between this opening and close, the book shows virtually no connection with the letter format, being theological exposition. Similarly, the book of Hebrews does not spring epistolary conventions on us until the final eight verses (13:18–25)! Nonetheless, throughout the book we find numerous interspersed direct addresses and appeals to the recipients, and these appeals resemble those other New Testament epistles rather than a theological essay.

What is the usefulness of the designation letter-essay? The first use is that it gives us the best possible label for the books of Romans and Hebrews. They contain letter-writing conventions at the bookends, while most of what appears in the rest of the books is not simply teaching material but teaching that is extensive and systematic. An essay sticks with a topic and uses sophisticated and detailed logic, and this is true of Romans and Hebrews.

Additionally, if we use the related category of *didactic letter*, we have a framework for assimilating the larger than normal space devoted to theological and moral instruction in numerous New Testament epistles. We would not call this teaching material an essay, since it is too loosely organized to merit that label, but certainly these didactic letters *have affinities to* what we call an essay, with the implications of detailed theological reasoning.

Missionary Letters

The original missionary letters were not the ones that we receive or that are circulated in our churches today but instead some of Paul's letters in the New Testament. A missionary letter bears the signs of having been written by a missionary, but more is implied than that. At least part of the letter is a report of missionary activity to recipients who are in some sense involved in the missionary's life and work. A regular feature of missionary letters is the report of the missionary's travels or travel plans. Commentary on the epistles has long used the category of travelogue as an ingredient in some of Paul's letters.

While the foregoing considerations apply to numerous New Testament epistles, a few are more thoroughly missionary letters than this. Philippians can be read as a missionary update letter, written by a missionary nearing the end of his missionary life. Several of Paul's epistles are strongly autobiographical, and as Paul reconstructs and defends his life we are aware that we are reading about the life of a missionary (see, e.g., 2 Cor. 1–2; Gal. 2–3; and 1 Thess. 2–3).

Administrative or Official Letters

The Roman world of New Testament times was a far-flung world empire. Additionally, the Romans placed a high premium on political organization. The central government was located at Rome, and a network of subordinate rulers radiated outward from this focal point. Throughout the New Testament we read about this network of rulers. It is no surprise that this milieu created an epistolary genre that we can call the administrative letter, which fell into two general categories.

One was written by a political officer to a subordinate ruler in an outlying region, giving instructions and encouragement to the subordinate. A synonym for the label "administrative letter" is "official letter" (written by an official to a subordinate). The other type has been present throughout history and is known as the governor's report, giving an update of conditions in an outlying region or asking for advice. The Old Testament book of Nehemiah is partly a governor's report.

These categories are useful for some of the passages that we find in the New Testament epistles. No claim is made here that we find political letters in their pure form, but rather two other things. First, we find passages in the epistles that have *affinities to* the administrative letters of the Roman world, so that things fall into place more clearly if we are aware of the genre of the administrative or official letter. Second, we can see something that we find throughout the Bible, namely, the adaptation of literary forms of the surrounding pagan culture to the religious purposes of the writers of the Bible.

Under the general umbrella of the official letter we find several subtypes. One is the letter of succession in which a "higher up" officer gives instructions to a junior person about how to name successors for positions under his watch. Another is the letter of advice in which the senior person passes on recommended action to his subordinate. The letter of advice often merges with the letter of encouragement, as the senior person voices support and commendation.

To apply this to the New Testament epistles, we can start at the broad level and observe that all of the New Testament epistles were written by apostles who were God's delegated witnesses to the gospel. They are spiritual officials in the church. We accordingly read the epistles in the spirit that what the authors of the letters wrote carries an absolute spiritual authority. It is not our prerogative to decide what parts we wish to accept. The epistles are official letters.

In addition to this general adherence of the epistles to the genre of the official letter, three epistles belong to the genre even more strongly. They are the "pastoral epistles" written by Paul to the young pastors Timothy and Titus. From start to finish, these three epistles read like an instruction manual to subordinates "in the field."

In all instances, including both the general tenor of all of the epistles (written by apostles on the authority of God) and the three Pastoral Epistles, the content of these letters resembles that of administrative letters in the classical world. The "elder statesman" encourages his recipients, instructs them, offers advice, commands, exhorts, and rebukes. Anyone who heard or read these letters would know how to proceed with the task of living the Christian life.

LEARNING BY DOING

This unit is designed to enable you to apply the principles that the chapter has covered. These principles discussed in this chapter correspond to a series of epistolary genres that are present in the New Testament epistles, as follows:

- circular letter
- personal letter
- family letter and letter of friendship
- letter-essay
- missionary letter
- administrative or official letter

The purpose of these categories is not to encourage you to pigeonhole New Testament epistles as belonging to just one of these genres but the opposite—to give you the freedom to see multiple strands in the a given epistle and thereby be true to the hybrid nature of these letters. With this serving as the foundation, your assignment is to see how many of the genres enter the following passages from the epistles, along with the specific ways in which each one that you choose is present. An underlying goal is to see how knowing the genres helps you deal with the passage better than if you did not know about the genres that are present. Here are specimen passages to find in your own Bible:

- Romans 3:21–31
- Philippians 4:10–23
- 1 Thessalonians 5:12–28
- Titus 1:1–9

Literary Genres from the Broader World of Literature

The preceding chapter dealt with epistolary genres, or types of letters. But that is only the beginning of what we need to know about the genres of the New Testament epistles. The writers of the New Testament epistles incorporated several important genres that belong to the broader world of literature and not specifically to letter writing (the subject of the preceding chapter).

Occasional Literature

The most comprehensive of these further genres is a category known as *occasional literature,* or *occasional writing.* This genre is operative when a piece of writing takes its origin from a specific event or occasion in the world of the writer. Of course there is always a personal occasion (in contrast to a public occasion) at work whenever an author writes something, but that is not sufficient to raise a piece of writing into the realm of occasional writing. Occasional writing springs from something that is going on in the external social or cultural situation of the author.

When applied to the New Testament epistles, the occasion is something that is happening in the life of the recipients of the letters. This context always involves a local church or group of believers and sometimes also encompasses specific individuals who are named. Often Bible commentaries are helpful in filling in the picture of what can be inferred to be the occasion, but the tendency of scholarly commentaries is to overdo this contextualizing and offer speculation as established fact. We need to start with the text of the letter, and often this tells us as much as we need to know (if not always as much as we would like to know).

Below are three passages from the epistles that let us know that the material is rooted in a specific situation or occasion:

- The seventh chapter of 1 Corinthians begins with the statement, "Now concerning the matters about which you wrote," and then the entire chapter gives commands for marriage and sex. Paul is obviously replying to a topic that has been raised in a letter from the Corinthian church.
- In the epistle to the Galatians, we read, "I am astonished that you are so quickly deserting him who called you in the grace of Christ and are turning to a different gospel. . . . O foolish Galatians! Who has bewitched you?" (Gal. 1:6; cf. 3:1). The letter to the Galatians was occasioned by a heresy that had gained steam in the church at Galatia. We can infer from the letter itself that the heresy was a version of "works righteousness," in which the claim was made that Christians needed to practice the Old Testament ceremonial laws in order to attain salvation.
- In Hebrews 10:23 we read, "Let us hold fast the confession of our hope without wavering, for he who promised is faithful." Even though Hebrews is predominantly an exposition of doctrine, there are interspersed passages like this in which readers are urged to cling to their faith.

We can infer that the occasion of this epistle is the threat that Christians would relinquish their faith and revert to Judaism in the face of persecution.

What are the implications of the occasional nature of many New Testament epistles for our understanding of them? The implications are huge.

First, the content of an epistle immediately falls into place when we grasp the occasion or situation to which the author is speaking. The book of Hebrews is an example. If we understand that the author is addressing readers who are in danger of relinquishing their Christian faith and reverting to Judaism, we understand why he writes an entire letter that argues for the superiority of Christ over all other beings and of the new covenant in Christ's blood over Old Testament foreshadowings.

Secondly, the occasional nature of the New Testament epistles proves that they are letters, not systematic theological treatises or essays. The most helpful explanation I have encountered on this subject is the following passage from a biblical scholar:

> Since they are letters, the writer assumes much as known and accepted by his readers. . . . The points argued and stressed are often not those of the greatest importance. . . . To most of the churches addressed, Paul was no stranger. . . . They knew his views on the great central facts; these he can take for granted. It is to show them their mistakes in the application of these central facts to their daily life, to help their doubts, that he writes. . . . Furthermore, many of the questions he discusses are those propounded by the perplexed church. He answers the question because it has been raised.[2]

---

2   Morton Scott Enslin, *The Literature of the Christian Movement* (New York: Harper and Row, 1956), 213–14.

This accords with a whole tradition of interpretation flowing from biblical scholar Adolf Deissmann (early twentieth century) that the New Testament epistles do not set forth systematic theology but are the authors' reflections on Christian belief and conduct *as occasioned by a specific situation.*

Diatribe

The classical genre of the diatribe exerted a strong and steady influence on the New Testament epistles, and we have missed a lot by being deprived of this information. In the background is the social prominence of traveling orators and speakers in the first-century Roman world. These speakers were often the best show in town. The diatribe was a form of street preaching or oratory (and some aspects of it perhaps also a form of classroom teaching).

As we will see in a later chapter, the New Testament epistles are a combination of two distinct styles. The dominant one is variously called the eloquent style, the polished style, or the high style. Intermingled with it, or played off against it, is an alternate style that is informal and conversational. These two styles are actually perpetual tendencies in human discourse through the ages.

The diatribe belongs to the informal style, and I can proceed best by simply listing the characteristics of the diatribe, with each trait accompanied by specimen illustrations from the New Testament epistles:

- *Dialogue with imaginary questioners or responders, sometimes portrayed as opponents or hecklers from the audience:* "But someone will ask, 'How are the dead raised?'" (1 Cor. 15:35). "But someone will say, 'You have faith and I have works'" (James 2:18).
- *Retort to the imaginary opponent in a combative way:* "You foolish person!" (1 Cor. 15:36). "Do you want to be

shown, you foolish person, that faith apart from works is useless?" (James 2:20).

- *Question-and-answer constructions, sometimes catechism-like or hammer-like in effect:* "Then what advantage has the Jew? . . . Much in every way" (Rom. 3:1–2). "What is your life? For you are a mist that appears for a little time and then vanishes" (James 4:14). "Shall I commend you in this? No, I will not" (1 Cor. 11:22).

- *Rhetorical question:* "Has not God made foolish the wisdom of the world?" (1 Cor. 1:20). "Does he who supplies the Spirit to you and works miracles among you do so by works of the law, or by hearing with faith?" (Gal. 3:5). (A rhetorical question is not asked to elicit information but as a way of stating what is already known.)

- *Rhetorical question as a transition to the next section:* "What causes quarrels and what causes fights among you?" (James 4:1, followed by a whole chapter that answers the question).

- *Adducing famous and representative figures from the past as examples:* "For this is how the holy women who hoped in God used to adorn themselves, by submitting to their own husbands, as Sarah obeyed Abraham" (1 Peter 3:5–6). "Woe to them! For they walked in the way of Cain and abandoned themselves for the sake of gain to Balaam's error and perished in Korah's rebellion" (Jude 11).

- *Use of analogy as a rhetorical device:* "There is one glory of the sun, and another glory of the moon, and another glory of the stars" (1 Cor. 15:41, with the author using these analogies to illustrate that a person's physical earthly body is different from the glorified resurrection body). "Look at the ships also; though they are so large and are driven by strong winds, they are guided by a very small rudder wherever the will of the pilot directs. So also the tongue is a small member, yet it boasts of great things" (James 3:4–5).

- *Aphorisms or proverbs*: "Godliness with contentment is great gain" (1 Tim. 6:6); "We love because he first loved us" (1 John 4:19). "Rejoice in the Lord always; again I will say, rejoice" (Phil. 4:4).
- *Satire*. Satire is an attack on vice or folly. Here is a passage of satire in a diatribe: "Come now, you rich, weep and howl for the miseries that are coming upon you. Your riches have rotted and your garments are moth-eaten" (James 5:1–2).

No claim is made that all of these features appear with equal frequency in the epistles, but only that they occur with sufficient regularity that we recognize them as familiar features.

These features produce an overall effect that is even more noticeable than the individual traits. The diatribe style is vigorous and colloquial. In place of the urbane and refined style of the formal and polished tradition, the diatribe is hard-hitting and combative. It does not soothe but ruffles, in the mode of an Old Testament prophetic book like Amos. The common formula "rough and ready" is appropriate, defined by a dictionary as "exhibiting rough vigor rather than refinement or delicacy." Here is a typical example of diatribe style: "I have been a fool! You forced me to it. . . . For I was not at all inferior to these super-apostles [sarcasm], even though I am nothing. . . . For in what were you less favored than the rest of the churches, except that I did not burden you [by requesting money]? Forgive me this wrong!" [sarcasm] (2 Cor. 12; 11, 13). Or this: "I wish those who unsettle you would emasculate [castrate] themselves!" (Gal. 5:12).

Autobiography

One of the letter types represented in the New Testament epistles is the personal letter in which the writer shares information about himself, as well as recent or long-past happenings in his life. By itself this does not warrant the label *autobiography*, but sometimes a New Testament letter writer self-consciously adopts the stance of formally rehearsing a part of his life as a way of illustrating or proving a larger point. There are two types of autobiography in the New Testament epistles. One is a brief passage interspersed in a letter—perhaps too brief to be called autobiography, but nonetheless accurately labeled with the adjective *autobiographical*. These passages serve several purposes.

One purpose is the writer's adducing his own life (or a specific aspect of it) as a model to follow. For example: "You, however, have followed my teaching, my conduct, my aim in life, my faith, my patience, my love, my steadfastness, my persecutions and sufferings that happened to me at Antioch, at Iconium, and Lystra—which persecutions I endured; yet from them all the Lord rescued me" (2 Tim. 3:10–11). As we read that passage twenty centuries later, we do not learn a lot about Paul, but the picture of a life nonetheless takes root as Paul's life for a moment comes alive as a model to be emulated.

Second, an epistle writer sometimes shares a bit of his life as a testimony, with the aim of proving the validity of the gospel. For example: "At my first defense no one came to stand by me, but all deserted me. . . . But the Lord stood by me and strengthened me, so that through me the message might be fully proclaimed and all the Gentiles might hear it" (2 Tim. 4:16–17). Such a passage has the force of a personal testimony.

Third, the writer of an epistle sometimes shares information about his life in order to elicit empathy or sympathy with his situation. Here is an example: "For we do not want you to be unaware, brothers, of the affliction we experienced in Asia. For we were so utterly burdened beyond our strength that we despaired of life itself" (2 Cor. 1:8).

All of the foregoing autobiographical elements are a continuous aspect of the New Testament epistles. They are so frequent, familiar, and brief that we do not think of them as autobiographical, but they are. In addition, there are four epistles for which we can use the word "autobiography." They are 2 Corinthians, Galatians (1–2), Philippians, and 1 Thessalonians (2–3). Much of this material recounts Paul's missionary career and his spiritual life (the story of what was happening at various stages within Paul).

A related genre needs to be brought into the mix as well, for both the fuller autobiographies listed in the preceding paragraph and the short autobiographical passages that we find interspersed throughout the epistles. This genre goes by the Latin name *apologia pro vita sua*, which means "defense of his life." Sometimes Paul defends himself against detractors. Even though 2 Timothy is not so directly autobiographical as the four books named above, if we accept that Paul writes this letter while on death row, it emerges as a retrospective letter in which Paul looks back over his life of Christian service and vindicates the life he has deliberately chosen as a follower of Christ and as a missionary. It is a defense of his life.

Farewell Discourse

The farewell discourse is a well-established biblical genre. Some examples include Moses's farewell addresses to his nation (Deut. 31–33), similar addresses by Joshua (Josh. 23–24) and Samuel (1 Sam. 12), and Jesus' Upper Room Discourse (John 14–17). The most general feature of a farewell discourse is that it is spoken or written by a notable figure to a family or followers as he contemplates his imminent death.

No single farewell discourse in the Bible contains all of the possible ingredients of the genre. The following list should therefore be assimilated as a menu of ingredients from which the author of a farewell discourse draws:

- a summoning of followers, either physically or in absence by way of a letter
- an announcement of approaching death
- a recollection of past association
- exhortations to remain faithful to a shared ideal and to past instruction
- revelation of future events
- predictions of woe and controversies, sometimes accompanied by warnings against false teachers or those who would betray the ideals of the group
- instructions regarding how to live a godly life in the absence of the writer after his departure
- prayers and blessings for those left behind.

These ingredients represent a farewell discourse.

There are two New Testament epistles that fall into place if we approach them with the features of the farewell discourse in mind. They are Philippians and 2 Peter. In addition, 2 Timothy was written while Paul was on death row, awaiting execution. As a result, we can read it like other farewell discourses as giving us the writer's "last words" on life.

What are the implications for interpretation? First, a farewell discourse is a specific manifestation of an even broader form known as "last words," also known as "famous last words." There is a sense of ultimacy about such an utterance, which we receive as the author's final statement about life. Second, if we know the list of ingredients in a farewell discourse, we have a roadmap that enables us to identify the individual elements in such an epistle and also a general framework for seeing how the elements fit together into a total package and situation. The letter is as it is because of the farewell context.

LEARNING BY DOING

The list of genres discussed in this chapter is the following:

- occasional literature
- diatribe
- autobiography
- farewell discourse

With this as a menu of options, scrutinize the following passages in your own Bible and see how one or more of the genres explains what you find in a passage:

- 2 Corinthians 7:2–16
- Galatians 3:1–9
- Philippians 2:12–24
- 2 Timothy 4:1–8
- James 2:14–26

Opening and Closing
in New Testament Epistles

L etters in every culture have an "envelope structure" or "bookend structure"—something that begins the letter and closes it, with the main part of the letter sandwiched between those boundaries. For lack of better terms, these two conventional parts of a letter can be called the opening and closing. The classical or Roman letters that were contemporaneous with the New Testament epistles had these components.

As this guided study to New Testament epistles now moves to a consideration of the five elements that make up the basic epistolary paradigm, we will be looking closely at the individual parts, starting with openings and closings. Initially these passages might seem predictable and perfunctory, but that is a comment on how we read them, not on their inherent qualities. Because the openings and closings of the New Testament epistles seem on the surface to all be the same, we tend to read them quickly and without giving them careful attention.

To correct this, we need to accept a very important principle: every part of a biblical text is important and has something for us. There is edification even in seemingly routine parts of New Testament letters. But we will never unlock these passages unless we accept that there is edification in every part. Once we agree to that premise, we will be surprised by what we find.

Openings

Before we begin to analyze the openings of New Testament letters, it will be helpful to have an example in front of us. Here is a simple example: "Paul, an apostle of Christ Jesus by the will of God, to the saints who are in Ephesus, and are faithful in Christ Jesus: Grace to you and peace from God our Father and the Lord Jesus Christ" (Eph. 1:1). Six aspects of such an opening have a claim to our attention: the components, the purpose, the effect, the adaptation that it represents from secular letters of the Roman world, implications for our reading and interpretation, and how the openings of the epistles might serve as a model for us today.

The Elements of the Opening

We should note first that the opening of a letter is technically called a *salutation*. The liability of using that term with the epistles is that in our own letters the salutation is very abbreviated, as in, "Dear Sir," or "Dear George." The openings of the New Testament epistles are much grander than that, and we need a term that will encompass all of the material. As illustrated by the opening verse of Ephesians (quoted above), a complete salutation in the epistles consists of three elements:

- the sender(s)
- the recipient(s)—the individual or group to whom the letter is addressed
- an initial greeting from the sender to the recipient

Each of these can be explored on its own.

While most of the epistles were authored by one person, several of them list multiple people as the senders: "Paul, an apostle of Christ Jesus by the will of God, and Timothy our brother" (2 Cor. 1:1); "Paul and Timothy, servants of Christ Jesus" (Phil. 1:1); "Paul, Silvanus, and Timothy" (1 Thess. 1:1 and 2 Thess. 2:1). What should we make of multiple authorship like this? It reinforces the corporate nature of the missionary work of the early church. A circular letter is public in its issues and tone, and multiple authorship conveys a similar quality.

A second thing to note about the statement of the sender of a New Testament epistle is that it is often accompanied by a stately epithet (title for a person). For example: "Paul, an apostle of Christ Jesus by the will of God" (Eph. 1:1). An epithet elevates the person who is named by it, but more important than this general effect is that epithets are carefully chosen to characterize the person. It is thus important to ponder the epithets that accompany the names of the senders of the New Testament epistles. This does not require consulting a Bible commentary or study Bible but simply taking the time to ponder the epithets and extract the obvious meanings.

A similar analysis of the recipient(s) of a New Testament epistle is required. Here is what follows the identification of Paul as the sender of the epistle to the Ephesians: "To the saints who are in Ephesus, and are faithful in Christ Jesus" (v. 1). As with the identification of the sender, an expanded identification like this of the recipients needs to be unpacked. It immediately elevates the recipients in our thinking, but beyond that we need to ponder the specific things that Paul wants to identify as his first priority, both to the original recipients and to us as latter-day readers. Our premise needs to be that nothing was thoughtless in the composition of the details of the New Testament epistles. Everything that is there is intended for our instruction and edification.

The third element in the opening of a New Testament letter is a greeting expressed by the writer to the recipient. Our own tendency in an efficiency-minded, text-sending age is to get right to the business at hand, but that degree of curtness did not appeal to the ancient mind. To be sure, in Roman letters the greeting was over almost as quickly as it began, consisting almost uniformly of a single word that can be translated as "greetings." This becomes changed in New Testament letters to the highly charged formula "grace and peace," usually accompanied by exalted religious sentiments. In the salutation to Ephesians that we have been using for illustration, it takes this form: "Grace to you and peace from God our Father and the Lord Jesus Christ" (v. 2).

Purpose of the Opening

The purpose of the openings of the New Testament epistles is partly to dispense information. For the business of the letter to proceed, everyone needs to know who is sending the letter, and to whom. In our own formal or "business" letters, we begin with the so-called inside address and then directly address our recipient ("Dear -----"). This exchange is like opening a gate; without it, neither the sender nor the recipient can proceed.

The first two elements in a New Testament letter (sender and recipient) incorporate this exchange, too, but repeatedly as this guide to the New Testament epistles continues to unfold, we will see that an element of "above and beyond" enters the picture. It is as though the authors of the New Testament epistles cannot proceed to the main point of the letter without already transacting an important spiritual mission, such as this: "May grace and peace be multiplied to you in the knowledge of God and of Jesus our Lord" (2 Peter 1:2). The purpose of this "add-on" to the sender-recipient identification is to serve notice that the overall purpose of a New Testament epistle is religious.

Effect of the Opening

The effect of the features of an epistolary opening flows directly from what has been said about the purpose of them, but it is important to throw the emphasis on the reader for a moment. C. S. Lewis has said about reading an epic that we must "be receptive of the true epic exhilaration." The same principle holds true for our reading of the New Testament epistles: we need to go with the flow and allow ourselves to be elevated in spirit by what the writer places before us.

Along with this affective transaction, we can see that a picture of the Christian life is being painted in the opening. There is an instructional effect as well as an uplift of spirit. For example: "Grace to you and peace from God our Father and the Lord Jesus Christ, who gave himself for our sins to deliver us from the present evil age, according to the will of our God and Father, to whom be the glory forever and ever. Amen." Certainly this catches us up in spirit and imagination, but a picture of who Christians are in Christ also emerges. This grand epistolary opening is nothing less than a brief theological primer.

Adaptation of Classical Openings

Everything that has been said above is evident from looking closely at the openings of the New Testament epistles, but some aspects will stand out even more clearly if we place these openings beside the letters of the Greco-Roman world that was contemporaneous with the writers of the New Testament. The literary term for this is *foil*—something that "sets off" an element in a text by being either a parallel or a contrast.

We can start with the parallels. The New Testament writers partly accepted the cultural and literary forms that were familiar in their world. They did not try to reinvent the obvious way to begin a letter, namely, sender plus recipient. Similarly, they realized that some form of personal greeting served an important purpose, as enshrined in the Greek word *chairein* ("greetings"). Sometimes the secular letters included a brief wish for good health or a statement of remembrance.

But compared to the cursory and perfunctory salutation of classical letters, the openings of the New Testament epistles are a veritable explosion. They completely overflow the boundaries of the classical model. The somewhat shallow "greetings" is replaced by the theological formula "grace and peace." These are theologically charged words, and by means of them the New Testament writers in effect impart a blessing from God on the recipients. Then we have the stately epithets by which the recipients are named, and often the "grace and peace" formula is expanded into an exuberant theological celebration and portrait of the Christian life. The openings in the classical letters are secular, while the openings of the New Testament epistles are spiritual.

Implications for Reading and Interpretation

The openings of the New Testament epistles confirm something that emerges every time we look closely at the literary forms of the Bible, namely, that the writers self-consciously wrote in an awareness of literary conventions. The writers of the epistles knew how a letter was expected to begin, and they embraced the conventions. The opening of an epistle serves preliminary notice on us that the author was a craftsman for whom features of literary form were important. Our awareness of that keeps growing as we read more and more of the ensuing letter.

Secondly, we have seen that the writers of the epistles load their openings with important material. We need to respond by reading slowly, by pondering, and by analyzing the theological content that the openings contain. The openings of the classical letters of the time are perfunctory, but the openings of the New Testament epistles are profound. We need to respect that profundity.

A Model for Our Own Letters

I do not wish to press the issue, but I think we might learn a lesson about letter writing even from the openings of the New Testament epistles. Modern modes of email and texting have accustomed us to curt openings—in fact, nonexistent openings. Might a touch of gracefulness be a form of Christian witness?

More conclusively, we know that the writers of the New Testament epistles wrote to fellow Christians. Presumably they would not have written in exactly the same way to unbelievers. Much of our own correspondence is likewise with Christians. If the writers of the epistles molded their letters to be spiritually uplifting, even in the openings, surely we can "borrow a page from that book" and find ways to make our own letters a spiritual encouragement.

LEARNING BY DOING

The opening of 1 Corinthians (vv. 1–3) will provide an excellent test case for what has been said above. You should begin by reviewing the material and drawing up your own working list of what to do with an epistolary opening. Then apply those categories to the following passage (1 Cor. 1:1–3):

> Paul, called by the will of God to be an apostle of Christ Jesus, and our brother Sosthenes, To the church of God that is in Corinth, to those sanctified in Christ Jesus, called to be saints together with all those who in every place call upon the name of our Lord Jesus Christ, both their Lord and ours; Grace to you and peace from God our Father and the Lord Jesus Christ.

Closings

If we have been surprised to see how much is packed into the openings of the New Testament epistles, we need to prepare ourselves for a great deal more in the closings, which are much more varied and expansive than the salutations. Some of them occupy an entire final chapter in our Bibles. The brief version of what constitutes the closing is "final greetings and benediction." That is not incorrect, but it names only what comes at the very end of the closing unit. A lot of additional material follows the body of the letter and precedes the final greetings and benediction, and this material needs to be considered part of the closing.

The game plan for analyzing the closings of the New Testament epistles is as follows: (1) the final greeting and benediction; (2) additional material in the closings; (3) implications for reading and interpretation.

Final Greeting and Benediction

The very end of an epistle is formulaic, meaning that it consists of conventional repeated statements known as formulas. These remind us of the openings of the epistles, especially the "grace and peace" formula. To illustrate, here are three concluding greetings and benedictions:

- "Greet one another with a holy kiss. All the saints greet you. The grace of the Lord Jesus Christ and the love of God and the fellowship of the Holy Spirit be with you all" (2 Cor. 13:12–14).
- "Epaphras, my fellow prisoner in Christ Jesus, sends greetings to you, and so do Mark, Aristarchus, Demas, and Luke, my fellow workers. The grace of the Lord Jesus Christ be with your spirit" (Philem. 23–25).

- "Greet all your leaders and all the saints. Those who come from Italy send you greetings. Grace be with all of you" (Heb. 13:24–25).

Some of the closings omit the greeting and have only the final benediction. Some of the epistles either incorporate a doxology into the closing (or end with it) instead of a benediction (e.g., Rom. 16:25–27; Heb. 13:20–21; Jude 24–25). Most important of all is that the closing of a New Testament letter sounds a note of closure and finality. We feel that the letter has decisively ended in the right way.

Added Material
The closing of some of the New Testament epistles consists only of the greeting and benediction, but other endings incorporate more. In modern-day terminology, much of this material goes by the name "housekeeping business" in which the writer makes arrangements of some type or other. Usually this section includes numerous named people. Here are two examples:

- The last chapter of Romans devotes sixteen verses to listing people whom Paul wishes the Roman Christians to greet for him (vv. 1–16), followed by final instructions to the readers of the letter (vv. 17–20). Then Paul sends greetings to the Romans from eight of his companions (vv. 21–23), followed by a doxology (vv. 25–27).
- The following units comprise the last chapter of 1 Corinthians: instructions about a collection that had been made for Christians living in Jerusalem (vv. 1–4); Paul's travel plans (vv. 5–9); instructions regarding how to treat Timothy when he visits (vv. 10–11); instructions involving four named Christians known to both Paul and the Corinthians (vv. 12–18).

What such extended closings show at once is that the summary formula "final greetings plus benediction" does not do justice to what we find in many of the epistles. Often we can see an interplay between convention and originality in the closing of a New Testament letter.

Additionally, even though some of the units in the closing consist of exhortation such as we might also find in the body of the letter, this material has a different feel when it appears in the last chapter. Positioned there, it reads like the final instructions that we place at the end of our own letters—closing thoughts, not the main business of the letter.

We noted earlier that when we set the exuberant spiritual content of the openings of the New Testament epistles alongside the cursory "greetings" of Greco-Roman letters, the latter seem shallow. The same is true of the closings of the New Testament epistles. Letters of the surrounding culture sometimes included a brief wish for good health for the recipient, and there is nothing unworthy about a wish for physical well-being. But that is decidedly inferior to the concluding benedictions and other spiritual material that appears at the end of the New Testament epistles.

Implications for Reading and Interpretation

Much of what needs to be said about the closing of New Testament epistles resembles what was said earlier about the openings of those same letters. We can begin by observing that the authors of the New Testament epistles wrote in an awareness of established conventions and rules for letter writing. This begets confidence that they were in command of their compositions. We sense a respect for literary form and expectation, and we might note that some scholars apply the adjective "liturgical" to the doxologies and benedictions that we find in the closings of these letters.

Second, the so-called housekeeping items show how rooted the New Testament epistles are in everyday living. The content of the letters is so religiously and spiritually oriented that we can easily get the impression that life was otherworldly for the authors. The closings of the letters bring us back to real life. For example, we learn that Paul needs books and a cloak to make life in prison bearable (2 Tim. 4:13), that John has written a brief letter because he expects to visit the recipients soon (2 John 12), and that young Timothy needs to be put "at ease" when he passes through Corinth (1 Cor. 16:10). It dawns on us as we read that the Christian life does not whisk us away to an ethereal world but requires us to practice the spiritual life in our everyday world.

Finally, a sense of life emerges as we read the "add-on" material, and we can learn from this and be inspired by it. For example, some of the epistles have an abundance of names in the closing material; from this we get a picture of how communal the Christian faith was back then, and how it should be for us now. The Christian communities in various cities were part of a close-knit network. Local congregations were continuously having people commended to them and being sent to them.

LEARNING BY DOING

Begin by casting a backward glance at the material presented above regarding the closing of New Testament epistles. Then see how that enables you to deal with the following closing from Hebrews 13:18–25:

> Pray for us, for we are sure that we have a clear conscience, desiring to act honorably in all things. I urge you the more earnestly to do this in order that I may be restored to you the sooner.

Now may the God of peace who brought again from the dead our Lord Jesus, the great shepherd of the sheep, by the blood of the eternal covenant, equip you with everything good that you may do his will, working in us that which is pleasing in his sight, through Jesus Christ, to whom be glory forever and ever. Amen.

I appeal to you, brothers, bear with my word of exhortation, for I have written to you briefly. You should know that our brother Timothy has been released, with whom I shall see you if he comes soon. Greet all your leaders and all the saints. Those who come from Italy send you greetings. Grace be with all of you.

The Thanksgiving in the
Letters of the New Testament

The epistolary unit that scholars have taught us to call "the thanksgiving" is one of five fixed components in New Testament epistles. It appears just after the opening salutation, greeting, and benediction. In fact, some scholars regard it as part of the letter opening instead of a separate unit. In order to preserve the usefulness of the labels *thanksgiving* and epistolary *body*, we should call elements of thanksgiving that appear in the body of a letter "praise or commendation" (see the next chapter for more on this).

The customary claim that the thanksgiving was an innovation not found in Greco-Roman models needs only a minor qualification. Classical letters did sometimes include a brief statement of thanks to the gods for deliverance from calamity, but it was so cursory and superficial that it cannot be regarded as the model on which New Testament writers built their magnificent thanksgivings. They in effect produced something new, growing out of their revolutionary new life in Christ.

The thanksgiving can be explored in terms of both form and content. This chapter will take up four topics—the structure, the content, the function or effect, and implications for interpretation and teaching.

Structure

The first thing to say about the structure of a thanksgiving is to note its position in the letter in which it appears. Not all epistles have a thanksgiving, but in the eleven that have one, it is positioned immediately after the salutation and opening benediction, as the following list confirms: Romans 1:8–15; 1 Corinthians 1:4–9; 2 Corinthians 1:3–7; Ephesians 1:3–14; Philippians 1:3–7; Colossians 1:3–8; 1 Thessalonians 1:2–10; 2 Thessalonians 1:3–4; Philemon 4–7; 2 Timothy 1:3–5; 1 Peter 1:3–9.

A small qualification needs to be made, namely, that the exuberance and the language of the thanksgiving sometimes carry forward into the next verses that are actually a prayer for the recipients but seem to be cut from the same cloth. Technically this add-on is a prayer, but no one will be misled if it is treated as part of the thanksgiving. (Having said that, I will also note that people are confused when teachers and writers misrepresent what is actually in the text.)

Before we generalize further about the genre, it will be helpful to have an example before us. Here is an excerpt from the thanksgiving in Philemon: "I thank my God always when I remember you in my prayers, because I hear of your love and of the faith that you have toward the Lord Jesus and for all the saints. . . . For I have derived much joy and comfort from your love, my brother, because the hearts of the saints have been refreshed through you" (Philem. 4–5, 7).

The essential feature of such a passage is signaled by the word by which the genre is known: it is a statement of thanksgiving. More specifically, it is a personal expression of what the writer is grateful for as he begins his letter. The thanksgiving thus has an *occasional* aspect to it, arising from the specific occasion of the author writing to the stated recipient. Its normal location immediately after the letter opening is thus entirely plausible.

At the heart of all the thanksgivings is a technique known as the *inventory*. This means that the writer lists a series of things for which he is grateful. It is equally accurate to say that the writer compiles a list of blessings (and I will note that some scholars use the word "blessing" somewhat interchangeably with the word "thanksgiving"). An inventory of blessings reminds us of the Old Testament psalms of praise, which likewise catalog the acts of God, chiefly his blessings.

In addition to the structure provided by the inventory, the thanksgivings have a stock formula at the beginning. Two formulas dominate: "I thank my God" or "I give thanks to my God," and "Blessed be the God and Father of our Lord Jesus Christ." The inventory then lists the things for which the writer is thankful or for which he blesses God.

Content

In contrast to the classical letters of the same era, the epistles do not praise God for physical health but triumphantly sound a spiritual note. The cause of rejoicing is solidly spiritual in the epistles. The thanksgivings, like the openings and closings, transport us to a spiritual level of reality.

This spiritual focus is couched in theological and liturgical vocabulary—God, Christ, hope, mercy, faith, redemption, and such like. Exaggerated claims that the thanksgivings foreshadow the style and content of the letter that follows are demonstrably untrue. They evoke an unchanging spiritual reality. For the most part, we could transpose the thanksgiving from one epistle to another with no change in the letter whatever.

At the level of content, a basic division exists in the thanksgivings of the New Testament letters. Some of them are an inventory of spiritual riches that believers have in Christ. Here the emphasis is on what God has done. If we put these thanksgivings into a composite whole, they are an ever-expanding vision of God's great acts of salvation and sanctification. They are a kind of theological primer on what God has done in Christ.

The second category lists the writer's thanks in regard to what the recipients of the letter have done and are doing. These thanksgivings function as a report of the spiritual lives of the recipients, as the writer rehearses what he has heard about those to whom he is writing. Here is a specimen passage: "We ought always to give thanks to God for you, brothers, as is right, because your faith is growing abundantly" (2 Thess. 1:3). Sometimes there is a note of remembrance as the writer recalls the faithfulness of a congregation to whom he ministered as a missionary. An overall picture emerges of the success of the early church in the world.

Function or Effect

The thanksgiving serves as a transition between the opening of an epistle and the body. The question naturally arises as to what function is served by a thanksgiving placed in that specific location. A leading authority on the epistles claims that the thanksgiving is not ornamental but introductory to the specific letter that follows. Those are not the only two options that we should consider (being merely ornamental or being a summary of the letter that follows). For anyone who is enticed by claims that the thanksgiving introduces the style and content of the letter that follows, I leave a simple challenge: see if you can make such a correlation, and if you can, proceed to substitute a thanksgiving from another epistle and see if anything changes.

The first effect that we need to highlight is lyricism. A lyric is a composition (usually a poem) that expresses strong feeling. A good lyric not only *expresses* feeling but *creates or awakens* it. The epistles have a *continuous* lyric undertow, but in the thanksgivings this erupts above the surface. The first function of the thanksgivings is thus affective. These passages are "feel good" passages that sweep us upward emotionally and spiritually every time we read them. They are a quick fix for an emotional low.

A second function is pastoral. Often the writer had been in a pastoral role over the recipients of the letter, but even when that is not true, he projects a pastoral tone in his letters. Some commentators speculate that Paul begins his letters in the same way that he began his sermons. The effect of the elevated thanksgivings is to call us to our higher selves as believers in Christ. Before the writers of the epistles get to the particular subjects (plural) of their letter, they want to call their listeners to first things. Pastoral encouragement is a leading function that gets unobtrusively transacted in these thanksgivings.

A third possible function is exhortation, though of a very sub-surface type. There can be no doubt that a certain picture of the ideal Christian emerges from the thanksgivings. Additionally, the inventory of spiritual treasures that believers possess in Christ has the effect of reminding readers of their spiritual identity. In the distraction of daily living, we tend to forget that we possess these treasures. The thanksgivings exhort us to be who we are in Christ.[3]

Implications for Interpretation and Teaching

There are literary genres that are great to read but pose problems for analysis and teaching. The thanksgivings are preeminently passages that we can simply read and be elevated by. Like the

---

3   I am reminded at this point of a series of BE Bible commentaries authored by Warren W. Wiersbe—*Be Free* (Galatians), *Be Confident* (Hebrews), etc.

psalm of praise, however, an inventory carries its meanings on the surface and leaves little analysis or interpretation to be done. Nonetheless, avenues exist for moving beyond description to interpretation and analysis, along the lines of the preceding discussion. Here are good questions to ask regarding a thanksgiving:

- Does this thanksgiving express thanks for the treasures that believers have in Christ or for the flourishing of the recipients in their spiritual lives?
- What model or ideal emerges that we can aspire to achieve in our own spiritual lives?
- What wake-up call or reminder does this thanksgiving express for me personally?
- The English poet William Wordsworth expressed the view that a lyric poem rectifies people's feelings, and John Milton similarly claimed that poetry "sets the affections in right tune." How is that true for you as you assimilate a given thanksgiving?
- How does this thanksgiving serve as a model for what we should value most in fellow Christians?

LEARNING BY DOING

With the foregoing chapter in your awareness and at your disposal, see how that information and methodology can be applied to the following specimen (1 Peter 1:3–9):

Blessed be the God and Father of our Lord Jesus Christ! According to his great mercy, he has caused us to be born again to a living hope through the resurrection of Jesus Christ from the dead, to an inheritance that is imperishable, undefiled, and unfading, kept in heaven for you, who by God's power are being guarded through faith for a salvation ready to be revealed in the last time. In this you rejoice, though now for a little while, if necessary, you have been grieved by various trials, so that the tested genuineness of your faith—more precious than gold that perishes though it is tested by fire—may be found to result in praise and glory and honor at the revelation of Jesus Christ. Though you have not seen him, you love him. Though you do not now see him, you believe in him and rejoice with joy that is inexpressible and filled with glory, obtaining the outcome of your faith, the salvation of your souls.

Paraenesis: Walking Worthy of the Lord

araenesis (pronounced para-NEES-us) is one of five set forms, or elements, in New Testament epistles. This Greek word means "exhortation" or "advice." The question that immediately arises is why the scholarly world has decided to use a Greek word instead of an English equivalent. The answer is that no English word has received acceptance. In most situations, we should simply use the intimidating word "paraenesis," but if we are teaching the epistles to a class where the word "paraenesis" would be an insurmountable obstacle, the substitute English label "list of moral commands" will work fine. For reasons that will appear below, simply to call a paraenesis a passage of exhortation is too broad and does not adequately denote a string of moral commands.

General Considerations

We need to begin with some very broad generalizations. The first is that paraenesis consists of moral commands. In turn, we should define morality as behavior or conduct in relation to one's fellow humans. A command is a directive that imposes an obligation to obey it. Not all commands are moral commands; they might be directives about personal life or about doctrine (a command to believe something). For example, in setting out the proper procedure for celebrating the Lord's Supper, Paul writes, "Let a person examine himself, then, and so eat of the bread and drink of the cup" (1 Cor. 11:28). That is a spiritual command to be obeyed individually, not a moral command involving our relations with other people. Paraenesis is a compilation of moral commands.

Moral commands permeate the New Testament epistles and are not limited to passages of paraenesis. The impulse to exhort is never far from the writers' minds in the epistles. Here is a typical example: "Bear one another's burdens, and so fulfill the law of Christ" (Gal. 6:2). And four verses later: "Let the one who is taught the word share all good things with the one who teaches" (v. 6). These are scattered individual moral commands. By contrast, the literary form of paraenesis is a cluster of moral commands presented in rapid-fire succession.

We should also acknowledge that there is a general rhetorical stance of exhortation in the New Testament epistles. Even when the mode is straightforward instruction rather than commands, we assimilate the instruction in the spirit that the writer is exhorting us to believe the instruction and put it into practice. This general hortatory spirit of the epistles is not the same thing as paraenesis, but we can profitably note that paraenesis fits into a prevailing atmosphere in the epistles.

If we need to distinguish paraenesis from the scattered commands and the general spirit of exhortation found in the epistles, we also need to avoid confusing it with lists of virtues and vices. At first these seem to be identical with paraenesis, but in paraenesis the thing that gets highlighted is a concentrated sequence of commands: "Let brotherly love continue. Do not neglect to show hospitality to strangers. . . . Remember those who are in prison" (Heb. 13:1–3). In a virtue or vice list, the thing that gets highlighted is the list of virtues or vices, and if there is an element of command, it is intermingled instead of being a rapid-fire sequence.

The foregoing distinctions are intended to set off paraenesis from certain other forms and tendencies found in the New Testament epistles. The goal is to preserve a sense of precision for the form known as paraenesis. But this is not intended to paralyze us about whether a given unit of commands is or is not a paraenesis. There are many interspersed sections of moral exhortation in the epistles, and no harm is done if we apply the principles of paraenesis to them. Nonetheless, the more generalized units of exhortation on a given subject read more like an essay-style exposition of an idea and lack the concentrated punch of paraenesis. Biblical scholars use the adjective "paraenetic" for such passages, not the noun form "paraenesis." We should also note that the undisputed examples of paraenesis tend to appear late in an epistle (though there are exceptions). In fact, some leading scholars speak of the "concluding paraenesis" in the epistles.

Such forms as paraenesis and virtue-and-vice lists and household codes (discussed below) were a familiar part of the surrounding classical world of the New Testament writers. Nonetheless, to make paraenesis a standard and expected component of a letter is something that the writers of the New Testament epistles added to the letter genre of the ancient world (something that is also true of the thanksgiving).

Defining Paraenesis

As we turn to an analysis of paraenesis as it appears in New Testament epistles, it will be helpful to have an example before us. Here as an excerpt from a longer paraenesis in the epistle to the Ephesians: "Be angry, but do not sin; do not let the sun go down on your anger, and give no opportunity to the devil. Let the thief no longer steal, but rather let him labor, doing honest work with his own hands. . . . Let no corrupting talk come out of your mouths, but only such as is good for building up, as fits the occasion, that it may give grace to those who hear" (Eph. 4:26–29).

The first thing we note is that the passage consists of a list or cluster of individual moral commands. Being commands, these statements are more than statements of advice or potential courses of action. They are uttered by an authority figure, and they require obedience. Such a list of commands sets a moral standard by which we can measure our current state, and it functions partly as a wake-up call to correct what is amiss in our moral lives.

The first obligation that we need to meet in regard to paraenesis is to recognize and name a passage of paraenesis when we come upon it. Paraenesis is not simply exhortation but a concentrated unit of exhortation packaged as a sequence of commands. It has a set-apart and self-contained quality that calls attention to itself. We need to recognize this and determine the boundaries of a given paraenesis. While the customary position of paraenesis is near the end of an epistle, it can appear earlier (e.g., 2 Tim. 2:22–26), so we need to be ready to identify paraenesis wherever it appears.

Interpreting Paraenesis

When we move from description to interpretation, we reach a fork in the road between reading a unit of paraenesis and teaching it to a group. The problem in regard to the latter is that a list of moral commands carries its meanings on the surface and does not lend itself to analysis. This is no problem in devotional reading, where we simply read the passage and let the meanings filter into our consciousness. But if we have a time slot to fill, mere reading of the passage will not suffice, nor does it live up to the requirement that Bible study and teaching need to move from a descriptive level to an interpretive and analytic level.

A starting point for analysis is to look for classifications among passages of paraenesis. For example, some units of paraenesis are collections of self-contained individual commands, while others show a degree of topical unity. Second Corinthians 13:11 exemplifies a topically unified paraenesis: "Finally, brothers, rejoice. Aim for restoration, comfort one another, agree with one another, live in peace; and the God of love and peace will be with you." The general drift is harmonious living with fellow Christians.

Another avenue toward analysis is to note the resemblance that the moral commands have with proverbs. In fact, some writers on the subject speak of paraenesis as a cluster of proverbs or maxims. Some of the categories of wisdom literature can thus be applied to paraenesis. For example, proverbs use a basic division of labor between commanding positive actions and forbidding other actions. The commands in paraenesis fall into the same dichotomy. Sometimes proverbs combine a command or prohibition with a reason for obeying it, and we can find the same thing in some of the commands that make up a unit of paraenesis. For example, the commands in Hebrews 13 are accompanied by a reason (beginning with "for") a total of seven times.

Similarly, if we look closely at a proverb or a command, we can often discern an underlying principle or value that is being affirmed. Thus the paraenesis found in Galatians 5:16–26 begins with the statement, "But I say, walk by the Spirit, and you will not gratify the desires of the flesh." The list of commands that follows is unified by the principle of sins of the flesh and the need to exercise various forms of self-control against them.

In addition to looking for classifications and unifying principles, we can take interpretation in an analytic direction by exploring possible contexts for a given passage. We need to begin with a very large qualification: biblical scholars regularly make strained and unsupportable claims to find a specific context for passages of paraenesis, and we need to resist that practice. Occasionally, but only rarely, we can see that a paraenesis correlates to the specific content of a given epistle. An example is 2 Timothy 4:1–5, where the commands relate specifically to Timothy's calling as a minister. Overwhelmingly, the inferred context is one of two other things—the general context of life in a fallen world where Christians need constantly to be vigilant against evil conduct and be diligent to counter it with what is good; and second, the cultural context of unbelief and paganism (whether ancient or modern), with the commands being an implied rejection of prevailing values and morality in society at large. To relate the commands in paraenesis to those two contexts (the fallen world and the surrounding culture) is a good analytic exercise.

Additionally, it is useful simply to ask on the basis of the passage what might have elicited these specific moral commands. This is an exercise of imagination: what existing situation (either individual or corporate) can we imagine might have led the letter writer to put this particular string of moral commands together? A complementary exercise is to ask what the effect would be personally and corporately if Christians (starting with ourselves) were to obey the moral prescriptions and prohibitions named in the paraenesis.

Household Codes

A special category of New Testament paraenesis is known as the *household code*. This genre lists responsibilities and duties for particular groups of people within families or households. It has become common to call such units a household code because the phraseology is similar to ancient legal or moral "codes" of conduct. These codes stipulate how members of a given social group must relate to each other.

The household codes in the New Testament epistles define the roles and duties of three relationships—husbands and wifes, parents and children, and masters and servants. In regard to the last of these, we need to be aware that in the ancient world servants were regarded as part of a household. Only by a certain latitude can we turn this into our familiar modern institution of employer and employee. With the paired items noted above, the structure is fixed, as the author first addresses one of the groups in the named pair and then the other—a wife's duties first, for example, and then a husband's.

There are four household codes in the New Testament epistles: Ephesians 5:21–6:9; Colossians 3:18–4:1; Titus 2:1–10; and 1 Peter 2:18–3:7. The latter two omit one or more of the six groups.

Why Paraenesis?

Paraenesis is not only a fixed form (expected ingredient) in New Testament epistles; its inclusion represents something that the writers added to the letter-writing conventions of the surrounding pagan culture. It is natural to draw conclusions as to why the writers made paraenesis an important part of their letters. Below are underlying principles that offer a plausible explanation of why paraenesis is present in the New Testament letters, and at the same time they describe the effect produced by paraenesis:

- Paraenesis shows that morality or ethics is an indispensable part of the Christian life.
- As an extension of that, it establishes that belief or doctrine must work itself out in action (with paraenesis often positioned after a section of doctrine).
- It shows that the Bible is a guidebook to Christian living.
- It holds before us the ideal of a well-ordered life in the three spheres of the individual, the family, and society.

- Especially if we consider that paraenesis was an innovative aspect of letter writing in the ancient world, it can be seen to serve the function of holding Christians to a higher moral standard than an unbelieving society accepts.

LEARNING BY DOING

To synthesize what this chapter has imparted, you should begin by browsing the chapter as a quick review. Then apply the principles and implied methodology either to Ephesians 5 (as located in your own Bible) or the following passage from Colossians 3:18–4:6:

Wives, submit to your husbands, as is fitting in the Lord. Husbands, love your wives, and do not be harsh with them. Children, obey your parents in everything, for this pleases the Lord. Fathers, do not provoke your children, lest they become discouraged. Bondservants, obey in everything those who are your earthly masters, not by way of eye-service, as people-pleasers, but with sincerity of heart, fearing the Lord. Whatever you do, work heartily, as for the Lord and not for men, knowing that from the Lord you will receive the inheritance as your reward. You are serving the Lord Christ. For the wrongdoer will be paid back for the wrong he has done, and there is no partiality. Masters, treat your bondservants justly and fairly, knowing that you also have a Master in heaven.

Continue steadfastly in prayer, being watchful in it with thanksgiving. At the same time, pray also for us, that God may open to us a door for the word, to declare the mystery of Christ, on account of which I am in prison—that I may make it clear, which is how I ought to speak.

Walk in wisdom toward outsiders, making the best use of the time. Let your speech always be gracious, seasoned with salt, so that you may know how you ought to answer each person.

Body: Giving Shape to New Testament Epistles

The units of the New Testament epistles that have been discussed thus far—opening, closing, thanksgiving, and paraenesis—are brief and well-defined. The largest part of an epistle is the body, which constitutes a distinct problem in analysis of the epistles, as experts on the subject acknowledge. The body of an epistle is amorphous and varied. It follows no set form. To analyze the specific theological and moral content of an epistle does not help us get a handle on the epistles as a genre, and additionally it would not fit the purpose of this guide, which is to explore the literary dimension of the New Testament epistles.

The approach taken in this chapter is to apply the categories that are sometimes offered as types of letters, such as a letter of persuasion, a letter of exhortation, and an informational letter. Those are not helpful labels for identifying the genre of an epistle because they are subject matter considerations and do not name genres or literary forms. But if we view these as categories of *what is happening at a given point in a letter* (instead of a comment on the overall genre of the letter), we can get good analytic mileage out of them.

The organizing principle for this chapter is to divide the content of the epistles into an anatomy of *types of material* that make up the body of an epistle. The goal is to provide a road-map for traveling through the central part of an epistle. This is best achieved not by thinking in terms of the author's purpose, or by delineating the specific subject matter of a given epistle, but instead by thinking in terms of the type of content that the writer places before the reader. Much of the time we can identify corresponding forms or techniques that accompany a given type of material, such as the command for persuasion and appeals (such as the "let us" formula) for exhortation.

Since some of the material is overlapping and capable of being considered in one category or another, it will be helpful to see the lay of the land at the outset. The categories that this chapter will explore are as follows:

- instruction or exposition
- command
- exhortation
- persuasion
- autobiography and personal news
- praise and rebuke
- prayer and request

These are broad categories and are not intended to preempt what a later chapter will call embedded genres like creed, hymn, and virtue-and-vice lists.

Instruction or Exposition

We rightly think of the epistles as imparting information to the reader. This information is a form of instruction or teaching.

It is presented to the reader dispassionately (though it may be combined with categories that appear below, such as persuasion or rebuke). Because the authors of the New Testament epistles are God's delegated apostles to the church, their instruction is authoritative and official, not subject to dispute or rebuttal.

Here is a typical passage of instruction: "But the day of the Lord will come like a thief, and the heavens will pass away with a roar, and the heavenly bodies will be burned up and dissolved, and the earth and the works that are done on it will be exposed" (2 Peter 3:10). That verse dispenses information about the end of earthly history and is a passage of instruction.

The word "exposition" introduces helpful additional nuances into the discussion. Exposition is explanation, and in this situation it implies explanation of ideas. In keeping with the nature of a letter, the writers of the epistles do not develop their ideas in the form of an outline of generalizations with supporting details, but rather as a person sharing more and more of his thinking on a subject. Here is a passage of exposition in which the author shares his process of thinking on the subject of Christian love:

> Anyone who does not love does not know God, because God is love. In this the love of God was made manifest among us, that God sent his only Son into the world, so that we might live through him. In this is love, not that we have loved God but that he loved us and sent his Son to be the propitiation for our sins. Beloved, if God so loved us, we also ought to love one another. (1 John 4:9–11)

The form in which instruction and exposition are embodied in the epistles is the direct, declarative sentence, as illustrated by the quoted passages.

What are the implications for interpretation? Instruction and exposition appeal to our minds. The writer's goal is that we understand the information that he dispenses and the process of thinking that he shares. Our responsibility is to make sure that we read carefully and understand what has been asserted.

Command

The rhetoric of command is much more prevalent in the epistles than we usually think. To confirm that statement, all we need to do is browse the epistles with an eye on the type of material that is presented (the format of this chapter). When we do, we will be surprised by how much of the material is presented as something that the writer is commanding us to do. Here is a specimen:

> Look carefully then how you walk, not as unwise but as wise, making the best use of the time, because the days are evil. Therefore do not be foolish, but understand what the will of the Lord is. And do not get drunk with wine. (Eph. 5:15–18)

That passage is a string of commands. Does such a passage instruct us in the Christian life? Yes, but it does not dispense information in the same way that a series of declarative sentences does, being more directive.

What are the implications for interpretation? A unit of commands does not function in the same way as the dispensing of information does. Its goal is to move us to obedient action, not simply grasping truth with our minds. There is an implied directive that we do something and not simply believe something.

Exhortation

To exhort is to utter urgent advice and strongly encourage someone either to believe an idea or to act in a certain way. An exhortation may register with us in the same way that a command does, but it is not phrased as directly. Here is an example: "Finally, then, brothers, we ask and urge you in the Lord Jesus, that as you received from us how you ought to walk and to please God, just as you are doing, that you do so more and more" (1 Thess. 4:1). Later in the same chapter we read, "But we urge you, brothers, . . . to aspire to live quietly, and to mind your own affairs, and to work with your hands, as we instructed you" (vv. 10–11).

One of the most customary means of exhortation in the epistles is the formula "let us," as in Galatians 6:10: "So then, as we have opportunity, let us do good to everyone, and especially to those who are of the household of faith." Or Hebrews 10:23: "Let us hold fast the confession of our hope without wavering, for he who promised is faithful." That is not exactly a command but rather an appeal designed to prompt us to behave in a certain way. Even when a writer does not use the format "let us," the effect of exhortation is to make us feel inclined to respond as the author has indicated. Ephesians 4:17 offers an example: "You must no longer walk as the Gentiles do, in the futility of their minds."

To take stock of what has been covered thus far, what makes up the body of a New Testament epistle? We are sometimes instructed, sometimes commanded, and sometimes exhorted. The goal of analyzing the body of an epistle according to this grid is to enable us to see what makes up the body of a New Testament letter.

Persuasion

Another type of material frequently found in the body of an epistle is persuasion. Persuasion may incorporate commands and exhortations, but its stance is to *move us* to assent intellectually or behave in keeping with the writer's desire.

Persuasion is not so much a rhetorical form as it is an author's intention in a given passage. The following example comes from the epistle to the Galatians, where Paul's whole thrust is to persuade his readers not to revert to the "works righteousness" of Judaism but to accept salvation as a free gift: "O foolish Galatians! . . . Let me ask you only this: Did you receive the Spirit by works of the law or by hearing with faith? Are you so foolish? Having begun by the Spirit, are you now being perfected by the flesh?" (Gal. 3:1–3).

There is a continuous persuasive cast to the New Testament epistles. Often it is intermingled with commands and exhortations as discussed earlier. It is true that much of the time we feel instructed as we read the epistles, but nearly as often we feel that we are being urged and persuaded to believe or do something.

The implications for interpretation are the same as with the other categories: we need to *identify* a unit in the body of a letter as being persuasive when that is the main business transacted in the unit, and then we need to *be persuaded* of what the author asserts and urges.

Autobiography

The genre of autobiography received treatment in an earlier chapter, but we also need to include it in the grid of ingredients in the body of an epistle. Autobiography is not simply an overall genre that is at work in the epistles but also an intermingled element. The reason we may overlook this autobiographical component is that it is so unobtrusive that it does not register with us as autobiography.

Here is an example of latent or easily overlooked autobiography: "But by the grace of God I am what I am, and his grace toward me was not in vain. On the contrary, I worked harder than any of them, though it was not I, but the grace of God that is with me. Whether then it was I or they, so we preach and so you believed" (1 Cor. 15:10–11). Paul is here talking about his own life and missionary career. Or this: "For we did not follow cleverly devised myths when we made known to you the power and coming of our Lord Jesus Christ, but we were eyewitnesses of his majesty" (2 Peter 1:16). Peter here recounts events from his life.

The implications for interpretation are at least twofold. First, we need to identify an autobiographical passage when it appears. Much of the autobiography in the epistles is so spiritually oriented that we do not realize that the author is writing about events in his own life. Second, to embody the spiritual life in concrete form like this is to obey a cardinal rule of literature, namely, that it is not abstract but enfleshed in physical forms. The implied lesson is that the Christian's whole life is spiritual in nature, even though it is lived out in the physical world.

In an earlier chapter, we noted that the closing of the epistles often includes "housekeeping" information about people or travel plans. When we find such passages in the body of the letter instead of the closing, we can simply call the units personal news, a type of autobiography. Here is an example: "I hope in the Lord Jesus to send Timothy to you soon. . . . I have thought it necessary to send to you Epaphroditus my brother and fellow worker and fellow soldier" (Phil. 2:19, 25). Paul is here writing about his personal life.

Praise and Rebuke

It is a regular feature of the epistles that the writers offer an assessment of the recipients of their letter or people they have observed. These assessments are an implied example from which we are expected to learn. Every time we encounter a passage of praise or rebuke, we should label it accordingly, realizing that it is as distinctive an element in the body of an epistle as the other categories named above are.

Here is an example of a passage of praise or commendation:

And we also thank God constantly for this, that when you received the word of God, which you heard from us, you accepted it not as the word of men but as what it really is, the word of God, which is at work in you believers. For you, brothers, became imitators of the church of God in Christ Jesus that are in Judea. (1 Thess. 2:13–14)

The counterpart is to hold a group up to rebuke for misconduct:

Come now, you rich, weep and howl for the miseries that are coming upon you. . . . You have lived on the earth in luxury and in self-indulgence. You have fattened your hearts in a day of slaughter. You have condemned and murdered the righteous person." (James 5:1, 5–6)

The first obligation for interpretation is to identify a unit as consisting of praise or blame. Then we need to operate on the premise of what literary scholars call *example theory*—the principle that authors put positive examples before us to emulate and negative examples to repudiate and avoid.

Prayer and Request

To make our grid complete, we need to add prayer and request. Occasionally the writer of an epistle utters a prayer or wish for the recipients of his letter: "May the Lord make you increase and abound in love for one another and for all" (1 Thess. 3:11).

Elsewhere the writers make requests of their readers or hearers: "Finally, brothers, pray for us, that the word of the Lord may speed ahead and be honored, as happened among you" (2 Thess. 3:1).

Summary

Experts on the epistles regularly acknowledge that although the body of an epistle is the largest component, it is the part that has received the least scholarly attention. The reason is that it is hard to get a handle on what constitutes the body of an epistle. The grid presented in this chapter offers a solution to that problem by enabling us to name the type of material that is presented, unit by unit, as we progress through an epistle.

Some scholars say that the body of a letter contains the main message, but this is rarely true of a letter and is misleading in regard to the New Testament epistles. The epistles, unlike an essay, do not have one central message but multiple individual messages. They are hybrids. The grid presented in this chapter allows us to see that and deal with it, at the same time alerting us to the unhelpfulness of the label "main message" for the body of the letter.

LEARNING BY DOING

The main types of material that are possible in a given unit of an epistle are as follows:

- instruction or exposition
- command
- exhortation
- persuasion
- autobiography and personal news
- praise and rebuke
- prayer and request

To see how this grid works itself out in an epistle, you can profitably analyze Philippians 1:12–4:20 as a specimen epistolary body.

Organization and Structure of New Testament Letters

T he brevity of this chapter should not be construed as a sign that the subject is unimportant. Much of the foundation has already been laid, and beyond that, the facts of the matter can be briefly stated. We then need to apply the principles of organization to every epistle as we come to it.

This chapter will explore three subjects: how we need to resist certain fallacies about the structure of the epistles; a review of data from earlier chapters that lay a foundation for seeing how the epistles are organized; and additional helpful tips for seeing the structure of individual epistles.

Fallacies

The most pervasive fallacy regarding the structure of the epistles is that they are structured like an essay or sermon. Several corollaries accompany those claims. One is that the epistles have a thesis statement. If we consult commentaries on the epistles we will quickly see a tendency of some scholars to identify a thesis statement for the individual epistles, usually consisting of a verse or two that come after the thanksgiving. These alleged thesis statements are either so generalized that they cover virtually anything that we might say about the Christian faith, or they name an idea that comprises only one topic among multiple ones that appear in the letter that follows. Choosing an early verse or pair of verses as a thesis statement misleads us into thinking that an epistle is unified around a single well-defined topic.

Almost as misleading is the common claim that each epistle has a "melodic line," or single unifying topic to which individual parts can be related. The result is reductionism in which a false unity is imposed on individual passages in an epistle. In sermons, this practice produces a series of monotonously repetitive sermons on an epistle. Nonetheless, the strategy of finding a melodic line holds promise if we realize that nearly all of the epistles have multiple melodic lines, and that some material in every epistle is extraneous to those melodic lines. For example, a large number of preachers and commentators claim that the unifying theme of Philippians is joy, so we can assume that this is one melodic line. But others believe that the melodic line is the concept of being in Christ and build their commentary around that interpretive slant. I believe that additionally some paragraphs in Philippians do not relate obviously to either joy or being in Christ.

Another fallacy is that the paragraphs in an epistle are seamlessly woven together by tight logical coherence. The result is that teachers and preachers make strained comments about how a given paragraph flows out of the preceding one. This impulse produces the tidy topical outlines of the epistles that we find in study Bibles and commentaries. In my research and writing on the epistles I have become skeptical of these outlines, and my skepticism grows as the amount of alliteration in an outline increases.

What all of the fallacies I have noted share is an unwillingness to do justice to the genre of the epistles. The epistles are letters, sharing the qualities of our own letters and emails. They are not essays or sermons. If we handed in an epistle as a paper in a theology course or read it from the pulpit as a sermon, we would be sternly judged as having confused our audience and failed to meet the conventions of an essay or sermon.

Despite my worries about misleading claims of unifying ideas in the epistles, I want to offer two qualifications. First, if an epistle is largely governed by a single topic, we should not suppress that fact but seize upon it. For example, 2 Thessalonians was written primarily to correct misconceptions about the two issues of the second coming of Christ and the need to work instead of being idle, but there is much additional material that does not relate to those two main topics.

Second, we need *some* unifying "big idea" under which to fit the content of the epistles. I myself find it useful to operate in an awareness that everything we find in the epistles teaches us about the Christian life, in its twofold aspect of telling us what Christians need to believe and what they need to practice as adherents of the faith. *Christian belief and living* are the melodic line of the epistles, both individually and as a group. That theme is broad enough to allow us to do justice to the diversity that we actually find as we progress through an epistle, and specific enough to provide focus and unity. The rubric "Christian belief and conduct" will help us chart our way through any epistle.

Review of Principles Previously Covered

The most pervasive structural principle for the epistles is the five-part paradigm that the writers obviously accepted as the agreed-upon template for an epistle. That paradigm is as follows:

- opening or salutation (author, recipient, greeting, grace and peace benediction)

- thanksgiving
- body
- paraenesis
- closing

With a given epistle, one of these elements might be missing or appear in an irregular place, but we will fare best if we begin with the expectation that this grid will organize an epistle.

When we come to the middle body of an epistle, our goal is to see and name what is actually before us, and not escape to an abstract framework removed from the text. A starting point for this is to identify the type of material into which a given unit falls. The possibilities are the following:

- instruction or exposition
- command
- exhortation
- persuasion
- autobiography and personal news
- praise and rebuke
- prayer and request

Of course we need to fill those categories with the specific topics that are discussed in these units, but we must start with the categories of form listed above, not with topical content. We need to say to ourselves that this unit is a prayer for recipients, this one a persuasive passage, this one a unit of commands, and so forth.

The Structure of Thought and Feeling

We come, finally, to the content of the units of an epistle. We need to accept the paragraph as the basic unit in the flow of thought or feeling in an epistle. The commonly repeated advice to "think paragraph" when we progress through an epistle is sound and will not let us down. Sometimes a paragraph will be related topically to the one before or after it, and much of the time it will not. The paragraphs themselves, though, are nearly always unified by a single idea or topic.

Before we place a paragraph into its immediate context, we need to make sure that we have grasped the paragraph itself. I am reminded of a formula that Victorian scholar Matthew Arnold bequeathed. Arnold said that in any field of intellectual inquiry, the goal is "to see the object as in itself it really is." We can never repeat that dictum too often, including when we progress through the individual units of an epistle.

Having stared at the paragraph under consideration, it is, indeed, important to ask what precedes it and what follows. Sometimes that context will be important to our analysis, and sometimes we will find that a paragraph is self-contained. We know right from the start that the opening thanksgiving and the concluding paraenesis are in the self-contained category. So are conventional inserts like the household code and virtue-and-vice list, or an inserted doxology or prayer. The impulse toward spontaneous insertion of material runs strong in the epistles, in keeping with the nature of letter writing and the strong emotions of the New Testament letter writers.

As for the flow from one paragraph to the next, we will benefit from accepting a structural principle that modern literature and literary criticism have popularized. It is called *stream of consciousness,* meaning that the sequence of thought that a writer puts before us follows the flow that happens within the human mind. The sequence might not be topical or logical but simply what happens inside people's minds. The jump might be disjointed because that is how the mind operates.

To sum up, the movement from one paragraph to the next in the epistles will fall into one of the following categories: (1) a logical movement from one idea to a related one; (2) a movement based on the occasion of the letter, with the writer answering questions that have been raised or subjects related to the circumstances to which the writer is responding; (3) the flow of consciousness in which the topic of a new paragraph is simply the next idea that came into the writer's mind during the process of composition.

LEARNING BY DOING

The foregoing discussion has laid down ground rules for the structure of an epistle viewed in terms of both literary genre (formal units) and content (topical units). A quick review of that material would be a good starting point for application. After that, while any New Testament epistle can be chosen for a learning-by-doing exercise, choosing a shorter rather than longer epistle is probably best. Colossians and Philippians are good candidates, but not the only ones. The book of James consists largely of proverbs and is too disjointed to be a good choice.

Embedded Genres within New Testament Epistles

Earlier chapters have discussed the overall genres that we find in the epistles. This chapter will delineate further genres that I have called "embedded" genres because they are found individually in the middle of other material. They resemble the thanksgiving and paraenesis in being self-contained genres with their own distinguishing traits. But the thanksgiving and paraenesis are forms belonging to the genre of the epistle, whereas the embedded genres discussed in this chapter are standard genres found beyond the epistles. We can think of these freestanding genres as having been imported by the letter writers into their epistles.

Lists of Virtues and Vices

The most numerous category of embedded genres is lists of virtues and vices, a form familiar in the surrounding classical world. It is a simple form accurately designated by the title. The main structural principle is the catalog or list. Here is a brief example (Col. 3:5, 12): "Put to death therefore what is earthly in you:

sexual immorality, impurity, passion, evil desire, and covetousness, which is idolatry. . . . Put on then, as God's chosen ones, holy and beloved, compassionate hearts, kindness, humility, and meekness."

With the basic format before us, we can make some elaborations. Sometimes lists of virtues and vices (or in the reverse order from that) are juxtaposed in the same passage, thereby forming a sharp antithesis—a kind of single combat between enemies. But at other times they are separated by intervening material, and at still other times one of them appears without the other in sight.

In all cases, the virtues and vices belong largely to the moral or ethical life, involving our relationships to fellow humans. They continuously remind us that correct belief is only one aspect of Christianity and that ethics is just as important as doctrine.

Usually the lists of virtues and vices are accompanied by an element of command to practice the virtues and avoid the vices. For example, the vice list called "desires of the flesh" in Galatians 5:16–21 is followed by the statement, "I warn you, as I warned you before, that those who do such things will not inherit the kingdom of God" (v. 21). Sometimes there is a direct command: "Pursue righteousness, faith, love, and peace" (2 Tim. 2:22).

How many virtue and vice lists do we find in the epistles? The approximate combined total is forty. Some are brief, and others are extended. Overall, it is a major genre within the epistles.

For devotional reading, we can let the lists filter into our consciousness and be edified and equipped to live the moral life. If we need to be analytic, below are some categories to apply. Some of the virtues and vices are individual, and others are communal and social. Some of the lists can be related to the context of the specific letter in which they appear, while others are interjected as part of general moral teaching. Asking why the writer placed a virtue or vice list in a particular place in a letter can yield insights. General theological themes can be explored, such as the depravity of the human condition with the vice lists and the sanctified life in connection with the virtue lists. Sometimes there is a unifying focus to a given list (such as sins of the flesh or variations on the theme of self-control).

Doxology and Benediction

A doxology is a command to praise God or an ascription of praise to God. Psalm 148:1 illustrates the format of commanding praise: "Praise the Lord." All of the fifteen doxologies embedded in the New Testament epistles use the formula "be," as in Romans 11:36: "To him be glory forever. Amen." Most the doxologies are brief like the quoted one, but sometimes they expand into something more exalted: "To the King of the ages, immortal, invisible, the only God, be honor and glory forever and ever. Amen" (1 Tim. 1:17).

The genre of the doxology sometimes merges into a certain type of benediction or ascription of blessing directed toward God (to be differentiated from the benedictions on people that appear in many openings and closings in the epistles). Here is one of five ascriptions of blessing to God in the epistles: "Blessed be the God and Father of our Lord Jesus Christ, the Father of mercies and God of all comfort. . ." (2 Cor. 1:3). Although the main purpose of the doxologies is affective or emotional, we should note that they also contain a doctrinal component from which we learn about the acts and character of God.

Four conclusions can be drawn regarding the doxologies and blessings of the epistles. First, a main theme of this guide to the epistles is to demonstrate the mixed-genre or hybrid nature of the New Testament epistles. In contrast to our own prosaic letters, the orientation of the epistles is toward expansiveness and exuberance as the writers reach out to encompass as much as their epistolary genre allows. A total of twenty doxologies/blessings plays its part in this exuberance over literary genres.

Second, doxologies have a formality and eloquence about them. They are at the opposite end of the stylistic continuum from colloquial, everyday speech. This is one of the stylistic strands in the epistles that we need to recognize and celebrate. When we come upon a doxology, we are swept up in the exaltation of the statement.

Additionally, doxologies and blessings are liturgical in nature. They were part of the storehouse of traditional formulas used by Christians in the first century. A point of ongoing debate for at least a century has been whether the New Testament epistles belong to the category of utilitarian correspondence used to transact the business of life or literary letters embellished by rhetorical and stylistic touches. The answer is that they are both, and the embedded genre of the doxology belongs to the literary or formal aspect of the epistles.

Finally, for all their exaltation and formal rhetoric, the doxologies thrust themselves forward in the epistles as a kind of emotional outburst. They are part of the incipient lyricism (emotional undertow) of the epistles.

Christ Hymn

Scholars speak somewhat loosely of hymns or "hymnic materials" in the epistles, but since there are only three undisputed hymns, and since all three are Christ hymns, we should use that label. A Christ hymn is a poem that praises the person and work of Christ. The writers of the epistles who work in this genre draw from the following menu of options: the praiseworthy acts and attributes of Christ, and the superiority or supremacy of Christ (often developed by contrasting Christ to something inferior). The three Christ hymns in the epistles are found in Philippians 2:5-11, Colossians 1:15-20, and 1 Timothy 3:16.

Encomium

An encomium is a poem or prose piece that praises either an abstract quality or a general character type. It is one of the most glorious genres in the Bible. The menu of motifs from which the writer of an encomium draws is as follows:

- introduction to the subject that will be praised, sometimes including a definition when the subject is an abstract quality
- the distinguished ancestry of the subject
- a catalog of the praiseworthy qualities and acts of the subject
- the indispensable or superior nature of the subject (often conducted by contrasting the subject to inferior rivals)
- a conclusion urging the reader to emulate the subject of praise

There are two encomia in the epistles: 1 Corinthians 13 in praise of love, and Hebrews 11 in praise of faith.

These two exalted encomia join the other embedded genres covered in this chapter in proving that the epistles are partly formal or literary epistles in which the artistry of composition mattered to the authors and therefore needs to matter to us as well.

Church Manual and Pastoral Handbook

A manual is an official directory of the procedures and methods of an institution or company. Churches have such manuals, and their original can be found within two New Testament epistles—1 Timothy and Titus. That Paul intended the former to be a church manual is evident from his statement in 3:15, where he claims to be "writing these things to you so that . . . you may know how one ought to behave in . . . the church of the living God." The guidelines in both 1 Timothy and Titus cover the following aspects of church life: qualifications for elders and deacons (1 Tim. 3:1–13 and 5:17–25; Titus 1:5–9); rules regarding widows (1 Tim. 5:3–16); and guidelines for older men and women, younger men, and bondservants (Titus 2:1–10).

A related genre that we can see in these two epistles is the handbook for pastors, instructing them how to handle various matters in their personal lives and in their relations with church members. This comes out most strongly in 1 Timothy 4:6–5:2 and 6:11–16.

With a little flexibility, we can add lists of church offices and gifts or roles within the church that are inserted into the epistles. These do not all name offices within the church, but they are catalogs that give us a picture of life within the church—not an official manual but a description that accurately delineates church life. Examples are Romans 12:4–8, 1 Corinthians 12:4–11 and 27–30, and Ephesians 4:11–12. The last-named passage reads, "And he gave the apostles, the prophets, the evangelists, the shepherds and teachers, to equip the saints for the work of ministry, for building up the body of Christ."

Travelogue

The travelogues in the New Testament epistles consist of news regarding past or intended future travels of the writer. Often the travel plans involve the recipients of the letter. Here is a specimen: "I hope to see you in passing as I go to Spain, and to be helped on my journey there by you, once I have enjoyed your company for a while. At present, however, I am going to Jerusalem bringing aid to the saints" (Rom. 15:24–25). A variation on the theme of the author's travels is information about an associate's travels, especially when Paul is "sending" that associate to the recipients of the letter.

Doubtless some of my readers will be surprised to find the travelogue elevated to the position of an embedded genre in the New Testament epistles. Is it sufficiently prominent to warrant that attention? It is. No fewer than fourteen of the epistles contain references to someone or other traveling or planning to arrive to visit the recipients of the letter. Most of these references are very brief, but a few are elaborated.

If these brief references seem not to merit the label *genre*, we at least need to put them on the agenda of *epistolary convention*—an expectation that the writers of the New Testament epistles nearly all incorporated into their letters. We can note three implications for interpretation.

First, the references to traveling confirm the international flavor of the New Testament epistles, which arose from the missionary nature of the early church. A vast network of contacts existed, and the epistles were part of that network.

Second, the presence of travel plans places the epistles into the genre of informal letter of correspondence intended to transact the mundane details of the writer and his recipients. This is one end of the genre continuum, with doxologies and Christ hymns and exalted thanksgivings at the other end (which we should call the literary epistle as distinct from informal correspondence).

Finally, the embedded travelogues create a very strong impression that the New Testament epistles are partly a substitute for person-to-person presence. Several times the writer confirms that he is writing because he is prevented from visiting, or that the letter is an interim measure that precedes an expected visit, as in the following example: "I had much to write to you, but I would rather not write with pen and ink. I hope to see you soon, and we will talk face to face" (3 John 13–14).

The starting point for this exercise is to review the genres that have been covered in this chapter. Then browse the following passages and identify the embedded genres found in them:

- 1 Timothy 3
- 2 Timothy 3 and 4

Style of the Letters
of the New Testament

tyle may seem of secondary importance for the epistles, but
it is not. Style is the form in which a writer packages the
content. It is the *how* of a discourse, and there is no *what*
(content) without the *how* (form). This is especially true of the
poetry and figurative language with which the New Testament
writers filled their letters.

Additionally, we need to accept the premise that whatever
we find in the New Testament epistles was composed by conscious design for our edification and pleasure. The writers did not
thoughtlessly happen to insert a poem or write an eloquent sentence replete with parallel clauses or include a list of virtues. All of
these were consciously placed into the letters. Everything that the
writers placed into the New Testament epistles under the superintendence of God is important. It was important to the authors,
and it needs to be important to us.

Poetry and Figurative Language

No aspect of the literary form of the New Testament epistles is more important than the poetic and figurative language that we find on virtually every page. The fact that this subject has not been discussed until the last chapter should not be allowed to obscure its importance.

Poets speak a language all their own. It is called *the poetic idiom.* Its essence is concrete imagery and figurative language. An image is any word naming a concrete action or thing. Much of the truth that poets express is embodied in images. The writers of the epistles were not poets but prose writers, but they continuously used the resources of poetry (as did Jesus in his discourses and sayings). We can say unequivocally that these prose writers *had a poetic side* to their temperament and practice as writers.

We can begin with the straight image, since it is the foundation of other figures of speech. The label *picture* is a good synonym for *image.* The impulse in literary discourse generally is not to be content with abstractions and generalizations but to give us pictures as well. In the following passage, Paul is not content to say "never avenge yourselves" but proceeds to give us pictures of that abstraction: "If your enemy is hungry, feed him; if he is thirsty, give himself to drink" (Rom. 12:19–20). In the Christ hymn in Colossians 1, we are not left with the abstract statement that by Christ "all things were created" but are given specific images of "things": thrones or dominions or rulers or authorities (Col. 1:16).

These remarks about images are only a "warm-up"; the really crucial poetic aspect of the epistles is comparisons in the form of metaphors and similes.[4] Both of these categories use the technique of analogy, and sometimes with an extended comparison (such

---

4   For more information about the use of imagery and how it works, see my previous volume in the series, *Sweeter Than Honey, Richer Than Gold: A Guided Study of Biblical Poetry* (Bellingham, WA: Lexham Press, 2018), ch. 2.

as the church as a body in 1 Cor. 12:12–20 and the complete armor of the Christian in Eph. 6:10–20) so that the word "analogy" seems most natural. A simile is a comparison that uses the explicit formula "like" or "as": "Like newborn infants, long for the pure spiritual milk" (1 Peter 2:1). Metaphor dispenses with the explicit formula "like" or "as" and makes a bold claim that A *is* B: false prophets "are waterless springs and mists driven by a storm" (2 Peter 2:17). Most pages of the New Testament epistles contain numerous metaphors like these.

Metaphors and similes need to be interpreted. That interpretation consists of analyzing how A is like B. First we need to make sure that we have a grip on level A. It is likely to be an image as defined above. Even before we carry over the meanings from A to B, we need to engage in interpretation of A. What is the literal image? What are its qualities that led the poet to compare the subject at hand to it? Then we need to carry over those meanings to the actual subject of the passage. In this regard, it is worth its weight in gold to know that the word "metaphor" is based on two Greek words meaning "to carry over." That is how to interpret a metaphor or analogy—carry over the meanings from level A to level B. Almost always the correspondences are multiple.

An example will clarify what I have said. First Thessalonians 5:5 gives us no fewer than five metaphors: "For you are all children of light, children of the day. We are not of the night or of the darkness." The first thing to do with a metaphor is identify it as such. There are actually five comparisons or metaphors in the quoted verse: Christians as children, as light, as day, and as different from night and darkness. The most important metaphor in the passage is the equation of a Christian with light. First we need to take time to name the qualities of light. Then we need to determine how those same qualities apply to being a Christian. Analogy in whatever form (including metaphor and simile) operates on the principle of using one area of human experience (level A) to explain or illuminate another area of experience (level B).

The writers of the epistles thought naturally in terms of analogy, metaphor, and simile. It was "second nature" to them. A figure of speech requires interpretation—and that entails time, meditation, and analysis. We cannot understand or teach the epistles well without taking the time and effort to interpret the figures of speech. The meaning resides in them.

High Style in the Epistles

Prose style exists on a continuum, ranging from the high style on one end to plain style on the other. To anticipate this chapter unit and the next, the prose style in the epistles combines both tendencies. Sometimes one comes to the foreground, and sometimes the other. This unit will explore the high style.

There are multiple terms by which literary critics name the high style. Here are some of them: "the grand style"; "the ornate or embellished style"; "the eloquent style"; "the polished style"; and "the formal style." These are all versions of the same stylistic quality. Writers of the high style do not want to reproduce the ordinary speaking voice but the opposite. They want to elevate language above its ordinary usage to correspond to the loftiness of the content and exalted occasion that produced the writing.

We should not mysticize the phenomenon of the high style. It is characterized by readily discernible traits, including the following:

- long sentences
- parallelism and balance of clauses or phrases
- repetition (in several potential forms)
- tendency toward exalted vocabulary
- regularity of rhythm (we hear the rise and fall of language in cadence)

- rhetorical forms such as antithesis, paradox, and epithet (an exalted title for a person or thing)
- figurative language (especially metaphor and allusion)

Not every passage of exalted prose includes all of these.

If we simply start to page around in the New Testament epistles, our eye will continuously fall on passages of high style. Here is a specimen (excerpt from 2 Cor. 6:4–10):

> . . . by great endurance, in afflictions, hardship, calamities, beatings, imprisonments, riots, labors, sleepless nights, hunger . . . ; with weapons of righteousness for the right hand and the left; through honor and dishonor, through slander and praise. We are treated as impostors, and yet are true; as unknown, and yet well known; as dying, and behold, we live . . . ; as sorrowful, yet always rejoicing."

This is a "fireworks" passage that incorporates all of the traits listed above. First, the entire passage (here only excerpted) consists of only two sentences, as the phrases keep piling up. The effect is exaltation. Repetition and parallelism or balances of phrases permeate the entire passage. Antithesis and paradox are present. The rhythm of words and phrases produces a cadence of rising and falling language. The vocabulary tends toward the formal and exalted. Metaphor makes an appearance with "weapons of righteousness." I did not go in quest for the passage quoted above; it was on my radar screen because I had just read it for personal devotions.

Something similar is true for the following passage (1 Tim. 6:13–16), and I share that personal information to confirm that the high style is continuously present in the epistles:

> I charge you in the presence of God, who gives life to all things, and of Christ Jesus, who in his testimony before

Pontius Pilate made the good confession, to keep the commandment unstained and free from reproach until the appearance of our Lord Jesus Christ, which he will display at the proper time—he who is the blessed and only Sovereign, the King of kings and Lord of lords, who alone has immortality, who dwells in unapproachable light, whom no one has seen or can see. To him be honor and eternal dominion. Amen.

All of the features of the high style are present here: long, flowing sentence structure; parallelism of clauses; exalted language; stately epithets (titles); allusion (reference to past history); regularity of rhythm (technically called cadence); and metaphor (keeping a commandment unstained).

What conclusions should we draw? First, there is an unwarranted bias in some circles against eloquence and the high style, which is perceived as being something that the biblical writers would not cultivate. The epistles refute that bias against the formal and eloquent on virtually every page. Eloquence is part of the artistry that we can admire in the epistles.

Once we accept that the high style is pervasive in the epistles, we can proceed to consider its effect. One effect is exaltation. The high style of the epistles fires our emotions and makes our imagination soar. We feel elevated and swept along. The eloquent style is one reason we find the epistles so memorable and why the phrases stick in our minds so that it is almost impossible to forget them. We should celebrate the high style of the epistles as one of their perfections.

At this point I need to say something about modern Bible translations. Essentially literal translations in the King James tradition retain the style of the original authors of the Bible. Modernizing translations depart from the original in two ways: the translators feel free to substitute words in place of what the authors wrote, and they make a decision right from the start to reduce everything in the epistles to a plain and simple style. The latter is an experiment in reductionism—reducing the length of sentences, the range of the vocabulary, and the figurative language (often even removing it). If we want to experience what God moved the writers of the epistles to write, the only way to do it is to avoid modernizing and colloquializing translations.

Plain Style in the Epistles

Two styles intermingle in the epistles. This combination makes the epistles unique. The high style makes us soar, and the plain style keeps us grounded in the everyday world where the events about which the authors wrote actually took place. The plain style is also known by such adjectives as "informal," "common," "colloquial," and "low" (not in disparagement but as the opposite of "high").

The high style aims to depart from everyday conversational prose. It does not want to reproduce the ordinary speaking voice but to transcend it. The plain style is the opposite of that. It aims to sound like the ordinary speaking voice. Its traits are accordingly the reverse of those that characterize the high style:

- short sentences and clauses
- common vocabulary
- frequent use of staccato effect rather than smooth rhythm
- absence of figurative language and rhetorical forms

Probably the writers of the epistles produced the plain style with neither more nor less conscious design than they produced the high style. As for the latter, Roman and classical culture was steeped in the high style, so it would be wrong to picture the writers as consciously producing a high-style passage and just unconsciously writing in the plain style. All of their stylistic choices were deliberate, and all of their choices (including 1 Cor. 13, the very touchstone of the eloquent style) seemed natural to them.

Here is a specimen of plain style prose from an epistle (1 Cor. 10:24–28):

> Let no one seek his own good, but the good of his neighbor. Eat whatever is sold in the meat market without raising any question on the ground of conscience. For "the earth is the Lord's, and the fullness thereof." If one of the unbelievers invites you to dinner and you are disposed to go, eat whatever is set before you without raising any question on the ground of conscience. But if someone says to you, "This has been offered in sacrifice," then do not eat it.

Despite the quotation from Psalm 24:1, this passage is conversational and largely devoid of the features of the high style.

Here is a second specimen (James 2:2–4):

> For if a man wearing a gold ring and fine clothing comes into your assembly, and a poor man in shabby clothing also comes in, and if you pay attention to the one who wears the fine clothing and say, "You sit here in a good place," while you say to the poor man, "You stand over there," or, "Sit down at my feet," have you not then made distinctions among yourselves and becomes judges with evil thoughts?

This passage approximates the ordinary speaking voice, with one exception, namely, that it is all one long sentence.

What conclusions should we draw regarding the plain style in the epistles? The first is that it is the minority voice. If we just start to page around in the epistles, we will find it relatively difficult to find plain-style passages. This is especially true if we factor in syntax or sentence structure, since the impulse toward parallel phrases and clauses, antithesis, and lists of things (a form of parallelism) is very strong in the epistles. When the plain style is present, however, it lends a quality that literary scholars call *realism*.

Some conventional components of an epistle tend to be in one style or the other. The opening thanksgiving, the interspersed prayers, and the doxologies are written in the grand style. The "housekeeping matters" and personal instructions that appear in the concluding chapter of some of the epistles tend to be in the colloquial style.

Aphoristic Style

An aphorism is a memorable statement or "catchy quotation" or "quotable quote." A book like *Bartlett's Famous Quotations* is a collection of aphoristic statements. The New Testament epistles are continuously aphoristic, and if we read them regularly we will find that many of the statements are familiar to us even if we have not memorized a passage.

Since approximately half of what I read in the epistles strikes me as aphoristic, I decided to check a specimen page of *Bartlett's Bible Quotations* as representing a more objective standard. Among the aphorisms from Philippians chosen by Bartlett are the following:

- "To live is Christ, and to die is gain" (1:21).
- "Work out your own salvation with fear and trembling" (2:12).
- "One thing I do: forgetting what lies behind and straining forward to what lies ahead, I press on toward the goal of the prize of the upward call of God in Christ Jesus" (3:13–14).

- "The peace of God, which surpasses all understanding, will guard your hearts and your minds in Christ Jesus" (4:7).
- "I have learned in whatever state I am to be content" (4:11).

The implications of the aphoristic flair of the writers of the epistles are very important. First, the aphoristic splendor stands as proof that the epistles are literary masterpieces whose technique can be admired. The epistles are both formal literary epistles and informal letters of correspondence. The aphorisms belong largely to the literary side. I need to qualify that last statement by saying that the informal style diatribe often incorporates proverbs.

Second, the aphoristic style of the epistles helps to explain certain features of them, and knowing this will help us understand what we see before us as we read the epistles. The memorability of the epistles stems in no small part from their aphoristic quality. This memorability can be an incentive to memorize passages from the epistles.

The profundity of the epistles also resides partly in their aphoristic presentation. An aphorism encourages us to ponder a statement and think about it in real-life situations. One of the most memorable sermons I ever heard has stuck with me since my grade school days; the aphoristic text for the sermon was, "For Demas hath forsaken me, having loved this present world" (2 Tim. 4:10, KJV).

LEARNING BY DOING

The main points covered in this chapter devoted to style have been poetry and figurative language, the intermingling of high and plain styles, and aphoristic tendency. The following passage will allow you to see how those stylistic traits converge in the epistles, and to analyze the passage accordingly (1 Cor. 15:51–16:4):

Behold! I tell you a mystery. We shall not all sleep, but we shall all be changed, in a moment, in the twinkling of an eye, at the last trumpet. For the trumpet will sound, and the dead will be raised imperishable, and we shall be changed. For this perishable body must put on the imperishable, and this mortal body must put on immortality. When the perishable puts on the imperishable, and the mortal puts on immortality, then shall come to pass the saying that is written:

"Death is swallowed up in victory."
"O death, where is your victory?
     O death, where is your sting?"

The sting of death is sin, and the power of sin is the law. But thanks be to God, who gives us the victory through our Lord Jesus Christ.

Therefore, my beloved brothers, be steadfast, immovable, always abounding in the work of the Lord, knowing that in the Lord your labor is not in vain.

Now concerning the collection for the saints: as I directed the churches of Galatia, so you also are to do. On the first day of every week, each of you is to put something aside and store it up, as he may prosper, so that there will be no collecting when I come. And when I arrive, I will send those whom you accredit by letter to carry your gift to Jerusalem. If it seems advisable that I should go also, they will accompany me.

Afterword

B ecause the epistles are mainly short books, it is possible to doubt the claim I made early in this book that the epistles are a hybrid form or mixed-genre form or encyclopedic form. To make sure that we do not lose our grip on the many-faceted nature of the epistles, it will be useful to review the multiplicity that has been covered in this book.

We should start with *types of letters* represented in the canon of New Testament epistles. The basic paradigm consists of five agreed-upon elements, which already signals a certain complexity. Then the list of partly overlapping types of letters keeps expanding: circular letter, personal letter, family and friendship letters, letter-essay, missionary letter, and administrative or official letter.

In addition to these *epistolary genres*, some important general genres appear prominently in the epistles. The most comprehensive is the genre of occasional literature: all of the epistles are more or less occasioned by some event or need in the first-century church. Also important are the diatribe, autobiography, and farewell discourse.

The constituents of the body of individual New Testament letters is even more dizzying: instruction or exposition; command; exhortation; persuasion; autobiography and personal news; praise and rebuke; and prayer and request. Even if a given letter contains just three of those, we can accurately speak of it as a hybrid.

Then there are embedded genres that writers imported into their letters. The list of these is substantial: lists of virtues and vices; doxology; Christ hymn; encomium; church manual; and travelogue.

Finally, stylistic considerations enter the picture. The writers continuously use the resources of poetry, especially metaphor. They are masters of both the high style and the plain style in the same letter. And the aphoristic tendency is so pronounced that it deserves study all by itself.

When we put all of those categories together, it is obvious that the epistles are hybrids and mixed-genre compositions. This makes them much more demanding than we often acknowledge, and it refutes the common misconception that they are essays and sermons. They are highly literary compositions and need to be approached as such.